왕초보 필수 영단어 960

초판인쇄 2018년. 11월. 10일.
초판발행 2018년. 11월. 15일.

펴낸이 편집부
펴낸이 진수진
펴낸곳 혜민교육

주소 경기도 고양시 일산서구 하이파크 3로 61
출판등록 2013년 5월 30일 제2013-000078호
전화 031-949-3418
팩스 031-949-3419
전자우편 meko7@paran.com

값 7,500원
*낙장 및 파본은 교환해 드립니다.
*본 도서는 무단 복제 및 전재를 법으로 금합니다.

영어를 여러 차원에서 기억하고 활용하는 방법인
영어 낭독 훈련을 통한 '스피킹 암기 학습'

초등 **영단어 960**은 영어 단어장이 아닙니다.
Shadow Speaking 332 학습을 기반으로 영숙어를 통해
영어를 익히도록 설계된 **신개념 학습법**입니다.

Shadow Speaking 332 학습 활용법

"과연 어떤 방법으로 연습하고 익히는 것이 효과적일까요?"
영어를 여러 차원에서 기억되고 활용하는 방법인 Shadow Speaking (낭독 훈련)을 통해 '스피킹 암기'가 가능하도록 연습하는 것

영어는 지능어가 아닌 기능어로 지속적인 노출과 기본 환경을 만들어주면 모국어를 익히는 것처럼 유창해집니다. 한국 사회에서 영어는 지능어로 인식되어 지식 수준으로 판단되어 온 것이 사실입니다. 세계어인 영어가 생존의 수단이요, 생활의 도구가 되었으며 이를 기반으로 사회가 변화고 교육 정책도 변화되면서 사람들의 인식에도 변화되어 가고 있습니다. 꾸준한 연습을 통해 유창성과 정확성을 기르면 누구나 영어를 잘 할 수 있다는 것입니다.

그렇다면 과연 어떤 방법으로 연습하고 익히는 것이 효과적일까요? 해답은 바로 영어를 여러 차원에서 기억하고 활용하는 방법으로 습득하는 것이 가장 좋은 방법일 것입니다. 바로 Shadow Speaking(낭독 훈련)을 통해 '스피킹 암기'가 가능하도록 연습하는 것으로 눈으로 보며, 귀로 듣고, 입으로 말하면서 영어의 기본기를 쌓는 것입니다. 소리 내어 공부하는 것이 다소 익숙하지 않을 수 있지만, 이것이 가장 빠른 Listening 훈련이요, Speaking 연습이며, 이를 통해 자연스럽게 영어의 발음과 화법을 효과적으로 터득할 수 있습니다. 무엇보다 Shadow Speaking(낭독 훈련)의 최대의 장점은 듣고 말하며 머리와 손으로 익히는 것이 아니라 눈과 귀와 입으로 익혀 원어민과의 실제 상황에서 익힌 것을 자연스럽게 표현할 수 있다는 점입니다. 즉, 살아 있는 실전에 강한 영어를 가능하게 해 준다는 것입니다.

영어는 어려운 수학 문제를 푸는 것처럼 지적 능력을 요구하는 학문이 아닙니다. 영어는 일상생활에 필요한 생활 언어이며 기능을 요하는 기능 교과입니다. 피아노 연습을 많이 하면 할수록 실력이 느는 것처럼 영어 또한 연습을 많이 하면 영어 실력자가 될 수 있습니다.

● Shadow Speaking 332학습 ●

Shadow Speaking 332학습은 낭독 훈련 원칙에 따라 일정한 학습이 이루어집니다. 즉, **오디오 3번 듣기**, **책을 보고 들으며 3번 따라 말하기**, **책을 보지 않고 들으며 2번 따라 말하기**를 해 보면서 익히는 것입니다. 눈으로 보며, 귀로 듣고 입으로 말하면서 영어 문장의 노출과 입력양을 늘려 실전에서 자연스럽게 암기한 내용이 표현되도록 하는 것입니다.

● 학습 결과와 피드백 ●

❶ **Shadow Speaking 332학습**은 듣고 연습하면 자연스럽게 입과 귀가 열려 듣기가 됩니다.
❷ **Shadow Speaking 332학습**은 말하는 연습을 통해 발음이 교정됩니다.
❸ **Shadow Speaking 332학습**은 듣고 말하며 머리와 손으로 익히는 것이 아닌, 눈과 귀와 입으로 익혀 실전에 강합니다.
❹ **Shadow Speaking 332학습**은 듣고 말하기 연습을 통해 영어의 유창성과 정확성을 기를 수 있습니다.
❺ **Shadow Speaking 332학습**은 영어 실력자들이 영어를 익혔던 학습법으로 결과가 검증된 방법입니다.
❻ **Shadow Speaking 332학습**은 다양한 교재를 통해 영어의 기초부터 기본기를 쌓을 수 있는 학습법입니다.

Shadow Speaking 332 초등 영단어 960

구성과 특징

Shadow Speaking 332 초등 영단어 960은 단지 영어 단어를 익히기 위한 영어 단어장이 아닙니다. 영어 학습을 하기 위해 영어 단어라는 텍스트를 바탕으로 특별한 영어 낭독학습(Shadow Speaking) 시스템을 통해 학습이 이루어집니다. 근본적으로 영어 단어를 통해 영어에 익숙해지고 영어 문장과 영영풀이를 통해 익혀 실전에 사용하기 위해서입니다.

초등 영단어 960은 가장 기본적인 초등 단어부터 빈도수 높은 중등 단어까지 다양하게 구성되어 있습니다. 학습 시스템은 Shadow Speaking 332학습법의 학습 흐름에 따라서 듣기, 말하기를 통해 자연스럽게 익히고 실전에 적절히 사용할 수 있도록 하였습니다.

Chapter 1 가장 기본이 되는 초등 단어들로 구성하여 단어와 문장을 통해 자연스럽게 학습하도록 구성하였습니다. (Spelling Bee 180 제공)

Chapter 2 중등 수준의 단어들로 빈도수 높은 단어들을 통해 실력을 다질 수 있도록 구성하였습니다. (Spelling Bee 100 제공)

Appendix 중등 단어들 중 240개의 빈도수 높은 단어들을 선별하여 영영풀이와 함께 제공하였고, 960개의 단어 색인을 통해 쉽게 찾을 수 있도록 하였습니다. 또한 Weekly Test를 통해 5일 학습 후 학습을 점검하도록 구성하였습니다.

* 초등 영단어 960+Key Word 240 = 1,200개의 단어 제공

학습 흐름

▶ 1. 영영단어 및 문장 듣기 3회 → 2. 영단어 및 문장 책보고 듣고 따라 말하기 3회 → 3. 영단어 및 문장 책 없이 듣고 따라 말하기 2회

- Shadow Speaking 332학습 원칙에 따라 듣기 3회, 따라 말하기1(책 보기) 3회, 따라 말하기2(책 없이) 2회를 기본 학습으로 실시
- 음성파일 : 듣기 파일과 따라 말하기 버전을 별도로 구성
- Unit별 1일 학습으로 학생들의 이해도를 고려하여 12개로 구성

초등 영단어 960은 영어 단어장이 아닙니다.
Shadow Speaking 332학습을 기반으로 영단어를 통해 영어를 익히도록 설계된 신개념 학습법입니다.

교재 구성과 특징

- 듣기용 음성 파일과 따라 말하기용 음성 파일을 구분하여 학습하는 데 있어서 학습효과를 극대화하도록 하였습니다.
- 각 영어 단어마다 체크 박스를 구성하여 스스로 확인하며 자기주도 학습이 가능하도록 하였습니다.
- 각 단어마다 영영풀이를 추가하여 영어식 사고를 통해 실력을 쌓도록 하였으며 More를 통해 동사변화나 비교변화 등을 제공하였습니다.

- Unit에서 익힌 영어 단어의 영영풀이를 각 Chapter별로 구성된 Spelling Bee를 통해 실력을 확인하고 점검하도록 하였습니다.
- Spelling Bee는 각 Chapter별로 구성하였는데, Chapter 학습이 끝난 후, 또는 Unit 학습 후 활용이 가능하도록 구성하였습니다.

- Appendix에는 Key Word 240 / Word List 960 / Weekly Test 등 다양한 자료를 제공하여 학습에 활용하도록 하였습니다.
- Key Word 240은 중등에서 빈도수 높은 단어 240개를 선별하여 영영풀이와 함께 제공하였습니다. 중등 시험에 자주 나오는 영영풀이 등에 활용하여 실력을 쌓도록 하였습니다.(초등 및 빈도수 높은 단어 960개+중등 빈도수 높은 단어 240=1,200 단어 제공)
- Weekly Test는 Unit 5회마다 1회의 주말평가 자료를 제공하였습니다.(Weekly Test 총 16회 제공) 이를 통해 학습이 끝난 후 점검하며 자신의 실력을 확인하도록 구성하였습니다.

Contents

* **Shadow Speakig 332 학습** 활용법 ---------------- 4
* 초등 영단어 960 구성과 특징 ---------------- 6

Chapter 1

초등 기본 영단어 ---------------- 9

unit	01	02	03	04	05	06	07	08
page	10	12	14	16	18	20	22	24
unit	09	10	11	12	13	14	15	16
page	26	28	30	32	34	36	38	40
unit	17	18	19	20	21	22	23	24
page	42	44	46	48	50	52	54	56
unit	25	26	27	28	29	30	31	32
page	58	60	62	64	66	68	70	72
unit	33	34	35	36	37	38	39	40
page	74	76	78	80	82	84	86	88
unit	41	42	43	44	45	46	47	48
page	90	92	94	96	98	100	102	104
unit	49	50						
page	106	108						

Spelling Bee 180 ---------------- 110

Chapter 2

빈도수 높은 영단어 ---------------- 123

unit	51	52	53	54	55	56	57	58
page	124	126	128	130	132	134	136	138
unit	59	60	61	62	63	64	65	66
page	140	142	144	146	148	150	152	154
unit	67	68	69	70	71	72	73	74
page	156	158	160	162	164	166	168	170
unit	75	76	77	78	79	80		
page	172	174	176	178	180	182		

Spelling Bee 100 ---------------- 184

* **Appendix** 1. Key Word 240 ---------------- 192
  2. Word List 960 ---------------- 206
  3. Weekly Test(총 16회) ---------------- 216
  4. Answers ---------------- 223

Chapter 1

초등 영단어 960은 영어 단어장이 아닙니다.
Shadow Speaking 332학습을 기반으로 영단어를 통해
영어를 익히도록 설계된 신개념 학습법입니다.

[초등 **600**
기본 영단어]
Unit 1~50

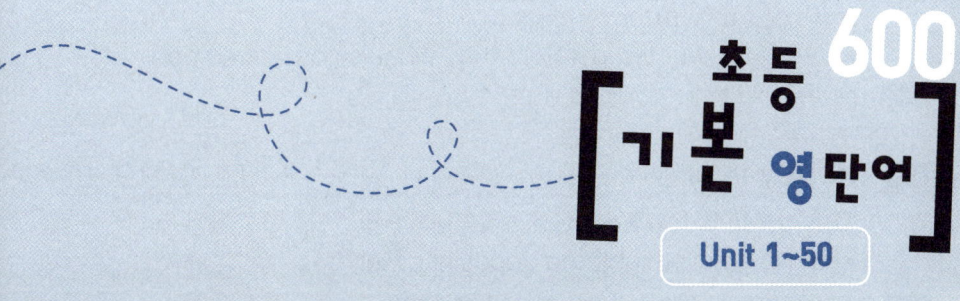

영단어와 문장, 영영풀이를 동시에 학습
Word 001~600

학습한 내용은 **Weekly Test**와 **Spelling Bee**를 통해
자신의 실력을 확인하며 익혀 보세요.

Shadw Speaking 332학습
① 오디어 3번 듣기
② 책을 보며 3번 따라 말하기
③ 책을 보지 않고 2번 따라 말하기

Listening
Speaking 1
Speaking 2

CHAPTER 1

Word 001~012

---

001 fever [fíːvər] 열

I had a fever yesterday. 나는 어제 열이 났었다.
▶ an illness where the body has a high temperature

002 cold [kould] 차가운, 추운

It is cold in winter. 겨울에는 춥다.
▶ having a lower temperature than what is considered cool

More have a cold 감기에 걸리다(cold 명사로는 '감기'), hot 더운

003 heavy [hévi] 무거운

This table is too heavy. 이 탁자는 매우 무겁다.
▶ having great weight; the opposite of light

More 비교변화 heavy - heavier - heaviest, light 가벼운

004 yesterday [jéstərdèi] 어제

We visited my grandparents yesterday.
우리는 어제 조부모님을 방문했다.
▶ the day before today

005 afraid [əfréid] 두려워하는, 무서워하는

I am afraid of dogs. 나는 개를 무서워한다.
▶ scared of something

006 diary [dáiəri] 일기

I keep a diary every day. 나는 매일 일기를 쓴다.
▶ a book that is used for writing down one's feelings and thoughts

UNIT 1

007 win [win] 이기다, 상을 받다

He won the marathon race. 그는 마라톤 대회에서 우승했다.
▶to be the most successful in a competition, race, etc.; to receive something for winning a contest

More 동사변화 win - won - won, winner 우승자

008 write [rait] 쓰다

Write your name on your book. 너의 책에 네 이름을 써라.
▶to put word on paper with a writing tool

More 동사변화 write - wrote - written, writer 작가

009 sand [sænd] 모래

The children were playing in the sand.
그 아이들이 모래에서 놀고 있었다.
▶a powder that is made of rocks and found at the beach or desert

010 beef [bi:f] 소고기

I like beef and vegetable soup. 나는 소고기와 야채 스프를 좋아한다.
▶meat from a cow

More pork 돼지고기, chicken 닭고기, fish 생선

011 towel [táuəl] 수건

Give me a towel. 수건 좀 주세요.
▶a piece of cloth used for drying

012 turn [tə:rn] 차례, 돌다

It's your turn. 네 차례이다.
▶a chance to do something that comes to each person in a group one at a time; to move around in a circle

CHAPTER 1

UNIT 02

Word 013~024

듣기 004, 말하기 005

013 wait [weit] 기다리다

Please wait for a moment. 잠시만 기다려 주세요.
▶ to stay in one place until one arrives

014 easy [íːzi] 쉬운

It is not easy to solve the problem. 그 문제를 해결하는 것은 쉽지 않다.
▶ not hard to do; not difficult

More 비교변화 easy - easier - easiest, difficult 어려운

015 cat [kæt] 고양이

A cat is chasing a mouse. 고양이가 쥐를 쫓아다니고 있다.
▶ a small animal with soft fur that people often keep as a pet

016 body [bádi] 몸

Wash your body first. 먼저 너의 몸을 씻어라.
▶ the physical part of a person or animal, including your head, neck, arms, legs, and trunk

017 there [ðɛər] 거기에, 그곳에

I want to go there. 나는 거기에 가고 싶다.
▶ in that place; in that location

018 oil [ɔil] 기름

Put some oil in the pan. 팬에 약간의 기름을 넣어라.
▶ a liquid that is greasy and used for cooking and making things like skin or car parts smooth, etc.

UNIT 2

019 **thing** [θiŋ] 물건, 물체

Can you pass me the thing over there?
저기 있는 물건을 나에게 건네주겠니?
▶ an item; an object

020 **park** [pɑːrk] 공원

They went to the park. 그들은 공원에 갔다.
▶ a place usually with grass and trees made for people to enjoy

021 **soft** [sɔ(ː)ft] 부드러운

My sofa is very soft. 나의 소파는 매우 부드럽다.
▶ feeling very smooth to the touch

More 비교변화 soft - softer - softest

022 **dollar** [dálər] 달러

Kate has ten dollars in her pocket.
Kate는 그녀의 주머니에 10달러가 있다.
▶ the standard unit of money used in the US, Canada, Australia, and other countries

023 **watch** [wɑtʃ] 보다, 손목시계

I watched TV in the evening. 나는 저녁에 TV를 보았다.
▶ to look at attentively; a device that shows what time is and that you wear on your wrist

024 **help** [help] 돕다, 도움

Help me, please! 도와 주세요!
I need your help! 나는 당신의 도움이 필요하다!
▶ to do something with or for someone to make the activity easier for him or her; aid

CHAPTER 1

UNIT 03 Word 025~036

Shadow Speaking 332

듣기 / 말하기1 / 말하기2

* 듣기 006, 말하기 007

025 outside [àutsáid] ~의 밖에

He went outside the house. 그는 집 밖으로 나갔다.
▶not inside; on the outer side of a building

More outside the gate 문 밖에, inside ~의 안에

026 desk [desk] 책상

The books are on the desk. 그 책들은 책상 위에 있다.
▶a table that is use to read, write and work

027 friend [frend] 친구

Tom is my close friend. Tom은 나의 친한 친구이다.
▶someone who you know and like very much and enjoy spending time with

028 pork [pɔːrk] 돼지고기

Today's lunch is pork. 오늘 점심은 돼지고기이다.
▶meat from a pig

029 pull [pul] 끌다, 당기다

The horses pull the carriage. 그 말들이 마차를 끈다.
▶to hold and move something toward you

030 ring [riŋ] 반지, (종, 벨이) 울리다

This ring is so pretty. 이 반지는 참 예쁘다.
▶a piece of jewelry that is worn around a finger; to make a sound with a bell

14 • Shadow Speaking 332

UNIT 3

031 chicken [tʃíkin] 닭

Chickens lay eggs every day. 닭은 매일 알을 낳는다.
▶a bird that is raised on a farm for its eggs and meat

032 rest [rest] 휴식, 쉬다

We took a rest at the beach. 우리는 해변에서 휴식을 했다.
▶time spent away from work or an activity; to relax

More take a rest 쉬다

033 fine [fain] 좋은, 맑은

It will be fine tomorrow. 내일은 날씨가 맑을 것이다.
▶all right; well; bright and not raining

More 비교변화 fine - finer - finest

034 fish [fiʃ] 물고기

There are many fish in the river. 강에는 많은 물고기들이 있다.
▶an animal that lives in water, and uses its fins and tail to swim

More 복수형 fish(여러 종류의 물고기들을 나타낼 때는 fishes)

035 bag [bæg] 가방

He put his lunch in the bag. 그는 그의 점심을 가방 속에 넣었다.
▶a container made of paper, cloth, or plastic used to carry things

036 away [əwéi] 떨어져서, 멀리

The lake is far away from here.
그 호수는 여기에서 멀리 떨어져 있다.
▶being apart from something

CHAPTER 1

UNIT 04

Word 037~048

Shadow Speaking 332

듣기 / 말하기1 / 말하기2

듣기 008, 말하기 009

037 can [kæn] 깡통, ~할 수 있다(가능)

We collected empty cans. 우리는 빈 깡통들을 모았다.
▶a metal container; to be able to do

038 arm [ɑːrm] 팔

Look at my long arms. 내 긴 팔을 봐.
▶the body part between the shoulder and the wrist

039 cook [kuk] 요리사, 요리하다

Cathy is a good cook. Cathy는 훌륭한 요리사이다.
▶a person who cooks; to prepare food by heating it

More cooker 요리 도구

040 rock [rɑk] 바위

Ann is sitting on the rock. Ann은 바위 위에 앉아 있다.
▶a large stone

041 book [buk] 책

I often read a book after dinner. 나는 저녁식사 후에 가끔 책을 읽는다.
▶a set of written or printed pages that are held together in a cover

042 weak [wiːk] 약한

My little brother is weak. 나의 남동생은 약하다
▶having little or no strength; the opposite of strong

More 비교변화 weak - weaker - weakest, a weak point 약점, a strong point 강점

UNIT 4

043 **afternoon** [ǽftərnúːn] 오후

I played soccer with my friends this afternoon.
나는 오늘 오후에 친구들과 축구를 했다.
▶ the time of day between morning and evening

044 **autumn** [ɔ́ːtəm] 가을

My favorite season is autumn. 내가 가장 좋아하는 계절은 가을이다.
▶ the season of the year between summer and winter and when leaves fall down and change color

More fall 가을

045 **square** [skwɛər] 정사각형

The cube is a square. 그 주사위는 정사각형이다.
▶ a rectangle with all four sides having the same length

More triangle 삼각형, rectangle 직사각형, circle 원

046 **after** [ǽftər] 뒤에, 다음에

I studied math after dinner. 저녁식사 후에 수학을 공부했다.
▶ at a time following; at a time later than

More after school 방과 후에, before 전에

047 **life** [laif] 생명, 삶, 생활

She has a happy life. 그녀의 삶은 행복하다.
▶ the state of living; the period during which one lives

More 복수형 lives / 동사형 live 살다

048 **miss** [mis] 놓치다, 그리워하다

He missed the bus. 그는 버스를 놓쳤다.
▶ to fail to catch or reach something; to feel sad because you can no longer see someone

CHAPTER 1

UNIT 05

Word 049~060

Shadow Speaking 332

듣기 / 말하기1 / 말하기2

※ 듣기 010, 말하기 011

049 **become** [bikʌ́m] (…으로, …이) 되다

Ice will become water. 얼음은 물이 될 것이다.
▶ to change into; to come to be

More 동사변화 become - became - become

050 **bicycle / bike** [báisikəl / baik] 자전거

I will ride my bicycle. 난 자전거 탈 것이다.
▶ a vehicle with two wheels that you ride by pushing its pedals with your feet

More Bike is short for bicycle.

051 **police** [pəlíːs] 경찰

I want to be a police officer. 나는 경찰관이 되고 싶다.
▶ people whose job is to keep the law

052 **into** [íntu] ~ 안으로

A man went into the house. 한 남자가 집으로 들어갔다.
▶ toward the inside of something

053 **put** [put] 두다, 놓다

Put the ball down there. 그 공을 거기에 내려놓아라.
▶ to place something somewhere

More 동사변화 put - put - put

054 **elephant** [éləfənt] 코끼리

The elephant has a long nose. 코끼리는 코가 길다.
▶ a large animal with a long nose

18 · Shadow Speaking 332

UNIT 5

055 **back** [bæk] 뒤로, 등

Go back to the house. 집으로 돌아가라.
- the rear side; the opposite of front; the part of the body between the neck and buttocks and opposite the chest and stomach

056 **tea** [tiː] (마시는) 차

I had a cup of tea. 나는 차 1잔을 마셨다.
- a drink that is made by putting tea leaves into boiling water

More green tea 녹차, black tea 홍차

057 **call** [kɔːl] …라고 부르다, 전화 걸다

We called him Tommy. 우리는 그를 Tommy라고 불렀다.
- to give a name to something; to reach someone by telephone

058 **summer** [sʌ́mər] 여름

It is the beginning of summer. 여름이 시작되었다.
- the warmest season of the year the season between spring and fall

More spring 봄, fall / autumn 가을, winter 겨울

059 **able** [éibəl] ~할 수 있는

I am able to go there. 난 거기에 갈 수 있다.
- to know how to do have permission to do; to be capable of doing

More be able to ~할 수 있다(= can)

060 **either** [íːðər] (부정문에서) …도, 역시

I don't like eggs. I don't like meat, either.
난 달걀을 좋아하지 않는다. 고기도 역시 좋아하지 않는다.
- likewise (used after a negative)

More too (긍정문에서) ~도, 역시

CHAPTER 1

Word 061~072

듣기 012, 말하기 013

061 run [rʌn] 달리다

I can run fast. 나는 빨리 달릴 수 있다.
▶ to move at a fast speed using the legs and feet; faster than a walk

More 동사변화 run - ran - run

062 glass [glæs] 유리, 컵

The glass is filled with juice. 그 컵에는 주스가 가득 차 있다.
▶ a hard, brittle material made from melting the clear part of sand

063 page [peidʒ] 쪽

Please open your book to page 7. 책 7쪽을 펴세요.
▶ one side of a piece of paper in a book other than the cover

064 backward [bǽkwərd] 뒤쪽으로(의)

Take a step backward. 뒤쪽으로 1걸음 걸어가라.
▶ moving toward the back; the opposite of forward

065 eye [ai] 눈

Open your eyes. 눈을 떠라.
▶ one of the two parts of your face you use to see

066 mouth [mauθ] 입

A hippo has a big mouth. 하마는 큰 입을 가지고 있다.
▶ the part of your face which you put food into, or which you use for speaking

20 · Shadow Speaking 332

UNIT 6

067 **old** [ould] 오래된, 나이 든

An old man is sitting on the bench. 늙은 남자가 벤치에 앉아 있다.
▶having existed or lived for a long time; the opposite of young

More 비교변화 old - older - oldest, young 젊은

068 **please** [pli:z] 부디, 제발, 기쁘게 하다

Please do this for me. 제발 나를 위해 이것을 해 주세요.
▶used to be polite when asking someone to do something; to make somebody happy

069 **excuse** [ikskjú:z] 변명하다, 용서하다

Excuse me for being late. 늦은 것을 용서해 주세요.
▶to overlook a mistake or wrongdoing

More Excuse me. 실례합니다.

070 **full** [ful] 가득 찬, 배가 부른

The box is full of books. 그 상자는 책들로 가득 차 있다.
I'm full. 배불러요.
▶having no empty space; satisfied with food or drink

More be full of …로 가득 차 있다, hungry 배가 고픈

071 **sell** [sel] 팔다

Thomas sells computers. Thomas는 컴퓨터를 판매한다.
▶to exchange something for money

More 동사변화 sell - sold - sold

072 **sky** [skai] 하늘

Ah, the sky is blue. 오, 하늘이 파랗구나.
▶the space around the earth where you can see the clouds

CHAPTER 1

UNIT 07 Word 073~084

Shadow Speaking 332

* 듣기 014, 말하기 015

073 puppy [pʌ́pi] 강아지

I am raising two puppies. 나는 강아지 2마리를 기르고 있다.
▶a baby dog

074 smell [smel] 냄새를 맡다, 냄새가 나다, 냄새

This flower smell sweet. 이 꽃은 좋은 냄새가 난다.
▶to use your nose to sense smells; a scent or odor that the nose can detect

075 ready [rédi] 준비된

Dinner is ready. 저녁이 준비되었다.
▶prepared to do something

More get ready for …에 준비하다

076 map [mæp] 지도

We looked at the maps in class. 우리는 수업 시간에 지도를 보았다.
▶a picture that shows how land is organized

077 hungry [hʌ́ŋgri] 배고픈

We are tired and hungry. 우리는 지치고 배가 고프다.
▶feeling of wanting food

More 비교변화 hungry - hungrier - hungriest

078 cookie [kúki] 과자

Can I have some cookies? 과자 좀 먹어도 되요?
▶a small baked food made of dough

UNIT 7

079 **capital** [kǽpitl] 수도, 대문자

Seoul is the capital of Korea. 서울은 한국의 수도이다.
▶ the city of a country where the government is centered; a letter of the form and size that is used at the beginning of a sentence or a name

080 **button** [bʌ́tn] 단추, 누름단추(버튼)

There are many buttons here. 여기에 많은 단추가 있다
▶ a piece of hard material that is sewn onto clothing and put into a hole in the clothing; a small part of a machine that you press to make it work

081 **cow** [kau] 암소, 젖소

Tom has seven cows. Tom은 젖소 7마리를 가지고 있다.
▶ a large farm animal that is raised for its milk and meat
More bull 황소, calf 송아지

082 **go** [gou] 가다

Let's go together. 함께 가자.
▶ to move or travel to a place
More 동사변화 go - went - gone

083 **nice** [nais] 좋은

The weather is really nice! 날씨 참 좋다!
▶ good; impressive; pleasant

084 **gold** [gould] 금, 황금

I have a gold ring. 나는 금반지를 가지고 있다.
▶ a valuable yellow metal that is often used to make jewelry

Word 960 • 23

CHAPTER 1

UNIT 08 Word 085~096

듣기 016, 말하기 017

085 chopsticks [tʃápstìk] 젓가락

He is still awkward with chopsticks. 그는 젓가락질이 아직 서투르다.
▶small sticks that are used in pairs to grasp food

086 spring [spriŋ] 봄, 샘물

Spring has come. 봄이 왔다.
▶the season between winter and summer when plants begin to grow; a place where water comes up from the ground

087 marry [mǽri] 결혼하다

He was 30 when he married. 그가 결혼했을 때 30살이었다.
▶to become someone's husband or wife
More get married to …와 결혼하다

088 carry [kǽri] 나르다

I will carry the books. 나는 그 책들을 나를 것이다.
▶to hold something while moving from place to place
More carry out 실행하다

089 very [véri] 매우, 아주

The weather was very nice. 날씨가 아주 좋았다.
▶to a high degree

090 thirsty [θə́ːrsti] 목마른

I'm thirsty. 나는 목이 마르다.
▶feeling the need to drink something

UNIT 8

091 **mouse** [maus] 쥐

That mouse is cute. 저 쥐는 귀엽다.
▶ a small furry animal with whiskers, round ears, and a thin tail

092 **week** [wi:k] 주

There are seven days in a week. 일주일은 7일이다.
▶ a period of seven days

More weekday 평일, weekend 주말

093 **tall** [tɔ:l] 키가 큰

You are very tall. 너 키가 참 크구나.
▶ having much length upwards

More 비교변화 tall - taller - tallest, short 키가 작은

094 **end** [end] 끝나다, 끝

The movie ends at ten o'clock. 영화는 10시에 끝난다.
▶ to finish; the last part of a period of time, event, activity, or story

More at the end of ~의 끝에, beginning 시작

095 **pay** [pei] 지불하다

I'll pay five dollars. 나는 5달러를 지불할 것이다.
▶ to give money for something you buy or for a service

More 동사변화 pay - paid - paid, pay for …의 대금으로 지불하다, payment 지불

096 **have** [hæv] 가지다, 가지고 있다

I have many toy cars. 나는 많은 장난감 차를 가지고 있다.
▶ to own; to be in possession of

More 동사변화 have - had - had, has 3인칭 단수형

CHAPTER 1

UNIT 09 — Word 097~108

듣기 018, 말하기 019

097 ship [ʃip] 배
We took a ship to Jeju-do. 우리는 배를 타고 제주도로 갔다.
▶ a large boat

098 shop [ʃap] 가게
I went to the toy shop. 나는 장난감 가게에 갔다.
▶ a place that sells things store

099 walk [wɔːk] 걷다
I walk to school. 나는 학교에 걸어서 간다.
▶ to move at a normal speed using the legs and feet
More take a walk 산책 나가다, go for a walk 산책하러 가다

100 church [tʃəːrtʃ] 교회
I go to church to pray. 나는 기도하기 위해 교회에 간다.
▶ a building made for paying respect to a god of a religion
More go to church (예배 보러) 교회에 가다

101 south [sauθ] 남쪽
Birds fly south in the winter. 새들은 겨울에 남쪽으로 날아간다.
▶ the direction that is right of the sunrise
More southern 남쪽의

102 balloon [bəlúːn] 풍선
My balloon is flying away! 내 풍선이 날아간다.
▶ a rubber bag that can be blown up

UNIT 9

103 send [send] 보내다, 발송하다

I sent a letter to him yesterday. 나는 어제 그에게 편지를 보냈다.
▶ to have something brought to a different from where the sender is

More 동사변화 send - sent - sent

104 loud [laud] 큰 소리의

You have a loud voice. 너는 목소리가 크구나.
▶ having much volume; noisy

105 take [teik] 타다, 잡다, 시간이 걸리다

She takes the bus to school. 그녀는 학교에 버스를 타고 간다.
▶ to get in a vehicle to go somewhere; to grab; to need or require a particular amount of time

More 동사변화 take - took - taken, take a picture 사진을 찍다

106 cousin [kʌzn] 사촌

I went to see a movie with my cousin.
나는 나의 사촌과 함께 영화 보러 갔다.
▶ a son or daughter of one's uncle or aunt

107 through [θruː] …을 통하여

We go into the building through the window.
우리는 창문을 통해 건물 안으로 들어간다.
▶ by way of; by means of

108 enjoy [endʒɔ́i] 즐기다

Jane enjoyed her vacation. Jane은 그녀의 휴가를 즐겼다
▶ to take pleasure in

CHAPTER 1

UNIT 10
Word 109~120

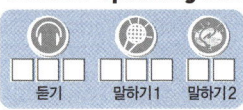
Shadow Speaking 332
듣기 / 말하기1 / 말하기2

듣기 020, 말하기 021

109 post [poust] 우편, 우편물
I mailed the letter by post. 나는 우편으로 편지를 보냈다.
▶ business dealing with mail delivery; letters, packages, etc. that are sent and delivered

110 leg [leg] 다리
Giraffes have long legs. 기린은 다리가 길다.
▶ the part of the body used for walking or running
More head 머리, arm 팔, hand 손, foot 발, knee 무릎

111 jeans [dʒiːns] 청바지
These jeans are too tight. 이 청바지는 너무 꽉 낀다.
▶ pants made of denim
More 항상 복수로 쓰는 것 : glasses 안경, scissors 가위, socks 양말

112 round [raund] 둥근
The earth is round. 지구는 둥글다.
▶ shaped like a circle or ball

113 girl [gəːrl] 소녀
She is a pretty girl. 그녀는 예쁜 소녀다.
▶ a young woman; the opposite of boy

114 team [tiːm] 팀
Our team won the game. 우리 팀은 경기에서 우승했다.
▶ a group of people who work together to play another or other groups of people

UNIT 10

115 **red** [red] 빨간, 빨간색의

Apples are red and bananas are yellow.
사과는 빨갛고 바나나는 노랗다.
▶ the color of roses or strawberries, etc.

116 **hot** [hɑt] 더운, 뜨거운

It is hot in summer. 여름에는 덥다.
▶ having a high temperature; the opposite of cold

More 비교변화 hot - hotter - hottest

117 **luck** [lʌk] 운, 행운

We finished it on time with luck. 우리는 운 좋게 제시간에 끝났다.
▶ good things that happen to you by chance, not because of your own efforts or abilities

More lucky 행운의, luckily 운 좋게, 다행히

118 **doll** [dɑl] 인형

Judy played with a doll. Judy는 인형을 가지고 놀았다.
▶ a toy that looks like a person

119 **wake** [weik] 잠깨다, 일어나다

I always wake up early in summer.
나는 여름에는 항상 일찍 일어난다.
▶ to get someone to stop sleeping; to stop sleeping

More 동사변화 wake - woke - woken

120 **meal** [miːl] 식사, 한 끼니

Eat balanced meals. 균형 잡힌 식사를 해라.
▶ the food served and eaten at one time

More have[eat] a meal 식사하다

CHAPTER 1

UNIT 11

Word 121~132

Shadow Speaking 332

듣기 022, 말하기 023

121 large [lɑːrdʒ] 큰, 넓은

We are a large family. 우리는 대가족이다.
▶big in size

More 비교변화 large - larger - largest

122 picture [píktʃər] 그림, 사진

There is a picture of a flower on the wall. 벽에 꽃 그림이 있다.
▶a drawing, painting, or photo of someone or something

More take a picture 사진을 찍다

123 toy [tɔi] 장난감

The baby plays with toys. 그 아기는 장난감들을 가지고 논다.
▶something for a person to play with

124 inside [insáid] 내부에, 실내(의)

My brother and I play inside on rainy days.
남동생과 나는 비 오는 날에는 실내에서 논다.
▶inner part of something

125 over [óuvər] ~을 넘어서

He jumps over the wall. 그는 담을 뛰어넘는다.
▶above and across something

More be over 끝나다, over there 저기 너머에

126 rice [rais] 쌀, 밥

I eat rice for dinner. 저녁으로 밥을 먹는다.
▶a seed of a cereal grass that can be eaten, especially in asia

UNIT 11

127 snow [snou] 눈, 눈이 내리다

The snow is melting. 눈이 녹는다.
▶ soft white pieces of frozen water that fall from the sky in cold weather; to fall as snow

128 sure [ʃuər] 틀림없는

I'm sure that you will do well. 네가 잘 할 수 있다고 틀림없이 믿는다.
▶ certain or convinced; not having any doubt about something

More be sure of ~을 확신하다

129 brush [brʌʃ] 빗, 빗다

My sister brushes her hair. 나의 언니는 그녀의 머리를 빗는다.
▶ a tool with bristles used to separate hair, paint, brush teeth, etc.; to move a brush through one's hair

130 die [dai] 죽다

Animals die without water. 동물은 물이 없으면 죽는다.
▶ to stop living

More 동사변화 die - died - died, dying 죽어가는

131 chess [tʃes] 체스(서양장기)

They are very interested in chess. 그들은 체스에 많은 흥미가 있다.
▶ a game that is played between two players with a checkered board and 16 pieces each

132 king [kiŋ] 왕

The lion is a king of animals. 사자는 동물 중의 왕이다.
▶ the male ruler of a country that is led by a royal family

More queen 여왕, prince 왕자, princess 공주

CHAPTER 1

UNIT 12 Word 133~144

Shadow Speaking 332

* 듣기 024, 말하기 025

133 size [saiz] 사이즈

What size do you want? 어떤 사이즈를 원하나요?
▶ the magnitude of something

134 thank [θæŋk] 감사하다

Thank you for calling me. 나에게 전화해 줘서 고마워.
▶ to show your appreciation to someone

More thanks to ~ 덕분에

135 gate [geit] 문, 정문

Many people gathered at the garden gate.
많은 사람들이 정원 정문에 모였다.
▶ a door which is set up to block the entrance of something

136 bottle [bάtl] 병

He has a bottle of milk. 그는 우유 1병을 가지고 있다.
▶ a container with a narrow neck used to hold a liquid

More a bottle of ~ 한 병

137 east [iːst] 동쪽

The sun rises in the east. 해는 동쪽에서 뜬다.
▶ the direction where the sun rises

138 hope [houp] 바라다, 희망

I hope you will be happy. 네가 행복하길 바란다.
▶ to desire for something to happen; a feeling that something good will happen

32 • Shadow Speaking 332

UNIT 12

139 sorry [sɔ́:ri] 미안한

I'm sorry. 미안합니다.
▶used to express regret

140 hotel [houtél] 호텔

They stayed at a hotel last weekend.
그들은 지난 주말에 호텔에 묵었다.
▶a building that has many rooms that people can stay at for one or more nights by paying money

141 fast [fǽst] 빠른, 빨리

Rabbits are so fast. 토끼는 매우 빠르다.
They run fast. 그들은 빨리 달린다.
▶at a high speed; going at a high speed

More 비교변화 fast - faster - fastest, slow 느린

142 both [bouθ] 둘 다의, 양쪽의

Both Jane and Mary are middle school students.
Jane과 Mary는 모두 중학생이다.
▶two things or people

More both A and B A와 B 모두

143 thumb [θʌm] 엄지손가락

She pressed her thumb on the paper.
그녀는 엄지손가락으로 종이를 눌렀다.
▶the short, thick finger at the inner side of the hand

144 zebra [zí:brə] 얼룩말

The zebra ran fast. 얼룩말이 빠르게 달렸다.
▶an animal that has black and white stripes and is like a horse

CHAPTER 1

UNIT 13 — Word 145~156

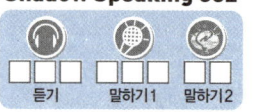

Shadow Speaking 332

듣기 026, 말하기 027

145 **bread** [bred] 빵

Can I have some bread? 빵 좀 먹어도 되나요?
▶ a food that is made from a mixture of flour and water and usually baked

146 **free** [fri:] 자유로운, 무료의

What do you do in your free time? 자유 시간에 무엇을 하나요?
▶ allowed to do or be anything; costing no money

147 **lamp** [læmp] 등, 램프

I have two lamps. 나는 램프를 2개 가지고 있다.
▶ an item that makes light, often covered by a shade

148 **duck** [dʌk] 오리

There are a lot of ducks in the pond.
그 연못에는 많은 오리들이 있다.
▶ a small bird with webbed feet that often swims in the water

149 **maybe** [méibi:] 아마, 어쩌면

Maybe he is sick. 아마 그는 아프다.
▶ perhaps; possibly

150 **center** [séntər] 중앙, 중심

My house is in the center of the town.
우리 집은 그 마을의 중심에 있다.
▶ the very middle of something

UNIT 13

151 answer [ǽnsər] 대답하다, 대답

The answer is correct. 그 대답이 맞다.
▶ to give a solution to a question or problem; something you say when someone asks you a question

152 zoo [zu:] 동물원

Last Sunday I went to the zoo with my family.
지난 일요일에 나는 가족과 함께 동물원에 갔다
▶ a place where animals are kept for people to see

153 subway [sʌ́bwèi] 지하철

We went to the amusement park by subway.
우리는 지하철을 타고 놀이동산에 갔다.
▶ an underground railroad that carries people around a city

More by subway 지하철을 타고(교통수단)

154 sun [sʌn] 태양

There is nothing new under the sun.
태양 아래에는 새로운 것이 없다.
▶ the large bright object in the sky that gives heat and light to the earth

155 money [mʌ́ni] 돈

My father gave me pocket money.
나의 아버지가 나에게 용돈을 주셨다.
▶ paper or coins used for buying and selling

More pocket money 용돈

156 see [si:] 보다

I saw a beautiful butterfly. 내가 아름다운 나비를 봤다.
▶ to notice with the eyes

More 동사변화 see - saw - seen, sight 시야

CHAPTER 1

UNIT 14 — Word 157~168

듣기 028, 말하기 029

157 pepper [pépər] 후추

Pepper is spicy. 후추는 맵다.
▶ a black powder used as a spice in foods

158 bad [bæd] 나쁜

It is bad to steal. 훔치는 것은 나쁘다.
▶ not good; the opposite of good

More 비교변화 bad - worse - worst, good 좋은

159 count [kaunt] 세다

My brother counted to ten. 나의 남동생은 10까지 셌다
▶ to say the numbers in order; to find the number of things involved

160 television [téləvìʒənl] 텔레비전

My father bought a television. 아버지는 텔레비전을 사셨다
▶ a device that enables you to watch moving pictures on a screen

161 welcome [wélkəm] 환영하다

Welcome to our home. 우리 집에 온 것을 환영합니다.
▶ to said to say hello in a friendly way to someone who has just arrived

162 knife [naif] 칼

He used a knife to open the box.
그는 상자 열기 위해서 칼을 사용했다.
▶ a sharp tool, usually made of metal, used for cutting

UNIT 14

163 **tiger** [táigər] 호랑이

The tiger is very strong. 호랑이는 매우 힘이 세다.
▶a large animal from the cat family that has fur that is light brown to orange in color with black stripes

164 **queen** [kwi:n] 여왕

The king and queen live in a castle. 그 왕과 여왕은 성에서 산다.
▶the female ruler of a country led by a royal family or the wife of a king

165 **new** [nju:] 새로운

I bought a new jacket. 나는 새 재킷을 샀다.
▶not old; recently made or obtained

More news 뉴스, old 오래된

166 **front** [frʌnt] 앞, 앞면

The building is in front of my house. 그 건물은 나의 집 앞에 있다.
▶the forward part of something a position ahead of something

More in front of ~의 앞에

167 **each** [i:tʃ] 각각의

Each student has a computer. 각각의 학생은 컴퓨터를 가지고 있다.
▶every one of two or more people

More each other 서로

168 **sour** [sáuər] 시큼한, 신

It is really sour. 그것은 정말 시다.
▶having an acid taste or smell like a lemon, etc.

More sweet 달콤한, salty 짠, bitter 쓴, spicy[hot] 매운

CHAPTER 1

UNIT 15
Word 169~180

Shadow Speaking 332

듣기 030, 말하기 031

169 too [tu:] 역시, 매우

He can play the piano, too. 그는 피아노도 칠 수 있다.
The cake is too sweet. 그 케이크는 매우 달다.
▶also; very

170 face [feis] 얼굴

Your face is beautiful. 너의 얼굴이 아름답다.
▶the front part of your head, where your eyes, nose, and mouth are

171 bear [bɛər] 곰, 낳다

Bears live in caves. 곰들이 동굴 속에서 산다.
▶a large and strong animal with thick fur, flat feet; to give birth

More 동사변화 bear - bore - born

172 cap [kæp] 모자

I wear a cap to protect my face from the sun.
나는 얼굴을 햇빛에서 보호하기 위해서 모자를 쓴다.
▶a kind of hat that often has a hard curved part that extends out over your eyes

173 chalk [tʃɔːk] 분필

My teacher writes with chalk. 나의 선생님은 분필로 쓰신다.
▶a writing tool made of a soft rock that is used on boards

174 may [mei] ~해도 되다, ~일지도 모르다

You may go home. 집에 가도 된다.
▶to be allowed to; to have permission to

UNIT 15

175 ill [il] 아픈

She is too ill to work. 그녀는 너무 아파서 일할 수 없다.
▶ not feeling well

More 비교변화 ill - worse - worst, well 건강한, be too ~ to 너무 ~해서 ~할 수 없다

176 market [máːrkit] 시장

I went to the market yesterday. 나는 어제 그 시장에 갔다.
▶ a place, often outside, where many kinds of things are sold by people

177 city [síti] 도시

Seoul is a big city. 서울은 큰 도시이다.
▶ a place where people live that is larger than a town

178 news [njuːz] 소식, 뉴스

Please tell me your good news.
나에게 너의 좋은 소식을 알려주세요.
▶ information about what just happened

179 yawn [jɔːn] 하품하다

He stood up, stretched and yawned.
그는 일어나서 기지개를 켜고 하품을 했다.
▶ to breathe by opening the mouth very wide, usually when tired or bored

180 smart [smaːrt] 영리한

She is smarter than her sister. 그녀는 그녀의 언니보다 영리하다.
▶ intelligent; well-educated

More 비교변화 smart - smarter - smartest

Word 960 • 39

CHAPTER 1

UNIT 16 — Word 181~192

Shadow Speaking 332

듣기 032, 말하기 033

181 **know** [nou] 알다
I know how to cook. 나는 요리할 줄 안다.
▶ to understand something fully
More 동사변화 know - knew - known, how to ~하는 방법

182 **toilet** [tɔ́ilit] 변기, 화장실
Where is the toilet? 화장실이 어디인가요?
▶ a device that has a seat, a bowl to collect human waste; bathroom or restroom

183 **ugly** [ʌ́gli] 추한, 못생긴
You are not ugly. 너는 못생기지 않았다.
▶ very unpleasant to look at, opposite of pretty
More 비교변화 ugly - uglier - ugliest

184 **always** [ɔ́:lweiz] 언제나
Jane always gets up at six. Jane은 항상 6시에 일어난다.
▶ at all times; every time

185 **find** [faind] 찾다
I found my key. 나는 내 열쇠를 찾았다.
▶ to discover; to come upon after looking for
More 동사변화 find - found - found

186 **tired** [taiərd] 피로한
I'm too tired and sleepy. 나는 너무 피곤하고 졸립다.
▶ having little energy; feeling a need to rest

UNIT 16

187 bee [biː] 벌

There are a lot of bees in the hive. 벌집 안에 많은 벌들이 있다.
▶a black and yellow-striped insect that collects pollen from flowers to make honey

188 basket [bǽskit] 바구니

There are a few apples in the basket.
그 바구니 안에 사과가 조금 있다.
▶a container made of strips of material like straw that are woven together

189 time [taim] 시간

We don't have a lot of time. 우리는 시간이 많이 없다.
▶the thing that is measured in minutes, hours, days, years etc. using clocks

More at that time 그때에, in time 제시간에, on time 정각에

190 late [leit] 늦은

I was late for school. 나는 학교에 늦었다.
▶near the end of a period of time; after the expected time

More 비교변화 late - later - latest, early 이른

191 all [ɔːl] 모든 것(의), 전부

I ate all of the ice cream. 나는 아이스크림을 다 먹었다.
▶everything; the whole

More after all 결국

192 some [sʌm] 조금의, 약간의

We have some food. 우리는 약간의 음식을 가지고 있다.
▶an unspecified amount or number of something; several; a few

More any 조금의, 약간의(some은 긍정문에 사용, any는 부정문·의문문에 사용)

CHAPTER 1

UNIT 17

Word 193~204

Shadow Speaking 332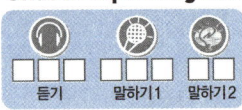

---

193 **box** [bɑks] 상자

The ring came in a beautiful box.
그 반지는 아름다운 상자로 왔다.
▶a stiff, usually rectangular container with or without a cover

194 **laugh** [læf] 웃다

He was laughing happily. 그는 행복하게 웃고 있었다.
▶to show joy or amusement with a smile and a chuckle or explosive sound

195 **kill** [kil] 죽이다

The cat killed the mouse. 그 고양이가 쥐를 죽였다.
▶to cause someone or something to die
More be killed 죽다

196 **cry** [krai] 울다

She cried out of sadness. 그녀가 슬퍼서 울었다.
▶to have tears come out of one's eyes

197 **student** [stjúːdənt] 학생

Many students study hard in the library.
많은 학생들이 도서관에서 열심히 공부한다.
▶someone who studies, especially at a school

198 **color** [kʌ́lər] 색깔

What is your favorite color? 가장 좋아하는 색깔은 무엇이니?
▶a quality such as red, blue, green, yellow, etc.

UNIT 17

199 **film** [film] 영화

He is a film actor. 그는 영화배우이다.
▶ a strip of plastic that can record pictures; a number of moving pictures coming one after another shown on a big screen, television, or through a video player or DVD

200 **piano** [piǽnou] 피아노

I can play the piano well. 나는 피아노를 잘 칠 수 있다.
▶ an instrument with black and white keys and three pedals that you can press to create music

More drum 드럼, cello 첼로, flute 플루트

201 **living room** [líviŋ ru:m] 거실

There was a sofa in my living room.
나의 거실에는 소파가 하나 있었다.
▶ a room in a house where people usually sit, talk, watch TV, etc.

More kitchen 부엌, bedroom 침실, garden 정원, bathroom 화장실

202 **zero** [zíərou] (숫자) 0

The score is five to zero. 점수는 5 대 0 이다.
▶ the number 0

203 **school** [sku:l] 학교

I go to school by bike. 나는 자전거로 학교에 간다.
▶ a place where teachers teach students

204 **west** [west] 서쪽

China is to the west of Korea. 중국은 한국의 서쪽에 있다.
▶ the direction in which the sun sets; the opposite of east

CHAPTER 1

UNIT 18 — Word 205~216

Shadow Speaking 332

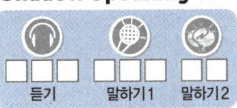

듣기 036 말하기 037

205 bird [bə:rd] 새

The bird is in the tree. 그 새가 나무에 앉아 있다.
▶an animal covered with feathers that has wings and a beak

206 hour [áuər] 시간

There are twenty-four hours in a day. 하루는 24시간이다.
▶60 minutes
More minute 분, second 초

207 lunch [lʌntʃ] 점심

It's time for lunch. 점심 시간이다.
▶a meal eaten in the middle of the day
More breakfast 아침식사, dinner 저녁식사

208 room [ru:m] 방

There are three rooms in my house. 우리 집에는 방이 3개 있다.
▶a part of a house that is divided from the rest of the house by walls

209 push [puʃ] 밀다

He is pushing the door. 그는 문을 밀고 있다.
▶to press against something in order to move it
More pull 당기다

210 white [hwait] 흰(색)

My chair is white. 나의 의자는 흰색이다.
▶the color of snow, milk, etc.

UNIT 18

211 that [ðæt] 저, 저것

That is a small car. 저것은 작은 자동차이다.
▶ a word used to refer to something or someone that is not close

More this: a word used to refer to something or someone nearby

212 get [get] 받다, 가지다

I got a toy airplane. 장난감 비행기를 받았다.
▶ to receive or come to have something

More 동사변화 get - got - got/gotten

213 tooth [tu:θ] 이, 치아

The baby has one tooth. 그 아기는 이가 1개 있다.
▶ one of the hard white things in your mouth that you use for eating

More 복수형 teeth

214 flower [fláuər] 꽃

She likes beautiful flowers. 그녀는 아름다운 꽃들을 좋아한다.
▶ a plant that has petals and leaves

215 aunt [ænt] 고모, 이모

My aunt is my mother's younger sister.
나의 이모는 내 어머니의 동생이다.
▶ a sister or sister-in-law of one's mother or father

216 big [big] 큰

There is a big table in my house. 나의 집에는 큰 탁자가 있다.
▶ large in size; the opposite of small

More 비교변화 big - bigger - biggest

CHAPTER 1

UNIT 19 — Word 217~228

Shadow Speaking 332

듣기 038 말하기 039

217 boy [bɔi] 소년

There are many boys on the playground.
놀이터에는 많은 소년들이 있다.
▶a young man; the opposite of girl

218 in [in] ~ 안에, ~에(시간)

The dolls are in the box. 그 인형들이 상자 안에 있다.
▶inside something; after a period of

More under ~ 아래에, on ~ 위에, by 옆에

219 tree [tri:] 나무

That tree is tall. 저 나무는 크다.
▶a woody plant that has branches and leaves

220 dog [dɔ(:)g] 개

The dog is barking. 개가 짖고 있다.
▶an animal that people often keep as pets, it is part of the canine family

More puppy 강아지

221 green [gri:n] 녹색(의)

The grass is green. 풀은 녹색이다.
▶the color of leaves, grass, etc.

222 small [smɔ:l] 작은

The rabbit is small. 그 토끼는 작다.
▶tiny or little; the opposite of big

UNIT 19

223 **other** [ˊʌðərt] 다른

They are the other team. 그들이 다른 팀이다.
▶the one besides this one; not the same

224 **today** [tudéi] 오늘

What day is it today? 오늘은 무슨 요일이니?
▶the present day

More yesterday 어제, the day before yesterday 그저께, tomorrow 내일, the day after tomorrow 모레

225 **chair** [tʃɛər] 의자

She is sitting on a chair. 그녀는 의자에 앉아 있다.
▶a seat with four legs and a back for one person

More sofa 소파, bench 벤치(긴 의자)

226 **work** [wəːrk] 일하다

They work Monday through Friday.
그들은 월요일에서 금요일까지 일한다.
▶to use strength or ability to get something done; to perform a job or duty

227 **minute** [mínit] 분

One hour is sixty minutes. 1시간은 60분이다.
▶an amount of time that lasts 60 seconds

More second 초, hour 시간

228 **beautiful** [bjúːtəfəl] 아름다운

You have a beautiful face. 너는 아름다운 얼굴을 가지고 있다.
▶pretty; delighting the senses

More 비교변화 beautiful - more beautiful - most beautiful

CHAPTER 1

UNIT 20 — Word 229~240

Shadow Speaking 332

229 happy [hǽpi] 행복한

I am happy with you. 나는 너와 함께 있어서 행복하다.
▶satisfied and joyful; glad

More 비교변화 happy - happier - happiest

230 same [seim] 같은

They go to the same school. 그들은 같은 학교에 다닌다.
▶similar in every way; having no difference

231 baby [béibi] 아기

The baby is playing in the room. 그 아기가 방에서 놀고 있다.
▶a very young child; a person who was recently born

232 daughter [dɔ́:tər] 딸

They have two daughters. 그들에게는 딸이 둘 있다.
▶a female child of a couple

More son 아들

233 fly [flai] 날다

Birds are flying in the sky. 새들이 하늘에서 날고 있다.
▶to move in the air without touching the ground

More 동사변화 fly - flew - flown

234 attack [ətǽk] 공격하다

The soldiers attacked the enemy. 그 군인들은 적을 공격했다.
▶to work against forcefully and violently

UNIT 20

235 many [méni] (수가) 많은

There are many cats. 많은 고양이들이 있다.
▶a large number of; a lot of

More much (양이) 많은

236 black [blæk] 검은(색)

My bag is black. 나의 가방은 검은색이다.
▶the darkest color

More white 흰(색), pink 분홍색, orang 주황색, brown 갈색

237 golden [góuldən] 황금의

I looked at the golden crown in the museum.
나는 박물관에서 황금 왕관을 보았다.
▶made from or covered with gold

238 woman [wúmən] 여자

She is a smart woman. 그녀는 똑똑한 여자이다.
▶an adult female lady; the opposite of man

More 복수형 women, men 남자(복수형 men)

239 people [pí:pl] 사람들

There are many people in the park. 공원에 많은 사람들이 있다.
▶a group of men; more than one person

More person 사람(복수형 persons), persons 대신 people을 흔히 사용

240 chest [tʃest] 가슴

Put your right hand on the chest.
당신의 오른손을 가슴에 놓으세요.
▶the part the body between the neck and the stomach area

CHAPTER 1

UNIT 21

Word 241~252

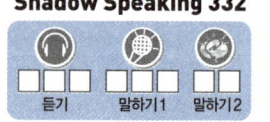
Shadow Speaking 332

듣기 042 말하기 043

241 apple [ǽpl] 사과

Apples taste sweet. 사과들은 단맛이 난다.
▶ a hard round fruit that has red or light green skin and is white inside

242 clothes [klouðz] 옷

Your clothes are beautiful. 너의 옷은 아름답다.
▶ the things that people wear to cover their body or keep warm

243 fun [fʌn] 재미

Playing is fun. 노는 것이 재미있다.
▶ producing enjoyment

More for fun 재미로, funny 우스운

244 clock [klɑk] 시계

Look at the clock. 그 시계를 봐라.
▶ an instrument other than a watch that shows the time

More watch 손목시계

245 harp [hɑːrp] 하프

The boy can play the harp. 그 소년은 하프를 연주할 수 있다.
▶ a large instrument with strings that is shaped like a triangle

246 fox [fɑks] 여우

The fox is smaller than the wolf. 여우는 늑대보다 작다.
▶ an animal like a dog that lives and hunts in groups

UNIT 21

247 man [mæn] 남자, 인간

He is a gentle man. 그는 친절한 남자이다.
▶an adult male; the opposite of woman

More 복수형 men, human 인간

248 wear [wɛər] 입다

I wear a shirt to go out. 나는 외출하기 위해 셔츠를 입는다.
▶to have on one's body, as in clothing or jewelry

More 동사변화 wear - wore - worn

249 young [jʌŋ] 젊은, 어린

He is young but very clever. 그는 어리지만 매우 영리하다.
▶having few years; the opposite of old

More 비교변화 young - younger - youngest

250 father [fɑ́:ðər] 아버지

My father often gives me pocket money.
나의 아버지는 종종 나에게 용돈을 주신다.
▶a male parent; dad

More parent 부모, mother 어머니, dad 아빠, mon 엄마

251 knock [nɔk] 두드리다, 노크하다

She knocked on the window. 그녀는 창문을 두드렸다.
▶to hit something with the knuckles of your hand or with a hard object to get people's attention

252 dentist [déntist] 치과 의사

I want to be a dentist. 나는 치과 의사가 되기를 원한다.
▶a person who cares for people's teeth, jaws and mouths

More doctor 의사, nurse 간호사

CHAPTER 1

UNIT 22 — Word 253~264

Shadow Speaking 332

듣기 044 말하기 045

253 blue [bluː] 파란(색)

My favorite color is blue. 내가 가장 좋아하는 색은 파란색이다.
▶the color of a clear sky or the ocean, etc.

254 teach [tiːtʃ] 가르치다

My teacher taught me to swim.
나의 선생님이 나에게 수영을 가르쳐주셨다.
▶to instruct; to help someone learn something

More 동사변화 teach - taught - taught

255 so [sou] 아주, 그래서

It is so cold. 아주 춥다.
▶very; and then

256 play [plei] 놀다, 경기하다, 연주하다

I sometimes play with a toy car.
나는 때때로 장난감 차를 가지고 논다.
▶to do something to have fun; to participate in a game or sport; to create sound with an instrument

257 cup [kʌp] 컵, 잔

I want three cups of coffee. 나는 커피 3잔을 원한다.
▶a container that is made for holding and drinking liquid

258 than [ðæn] ~보다

I am taller than my brother. 나는 나의 형보다 키가 더 크다.
▶a word used when comparing things

UNIT 22

259 **river** [rívər] 강

We are swimming in the river. 우리는 강에서 수영을 하고 있다.
▶ a fairly large stream of water

More stream river보다 작은 하천, brook 시내(개울)

260 **set** [set] 세트, 놓다

That's a nice gift set. 저것은 멋진 선물 세트이다.
▶ a group of things that are put together so that they can be used together; to put in a place

More 동사변화 set - set - set

261 **sad** [sæd] 슬픈

I am sad about losing my cap. 나는 모자를 잊어버려서 슬프다.
▶ showing grief and unhappiness; the opposite of happy

More 비교변화 sad - sader - sadest

262 **light** [lait] 전등

He turned on the light. 그는 전등을 켰다.
▶ an object that produces light by using electricity, oil, or gas weighing little

263 **sugar** [ʃúgər] 설탕

I want two sugars in my coffee.
나의 커피에 설탕 2개 넣어주세요.
▶ a sweet powder that is used to make food

264 **strong** [strɔ(:)ŋ] 강한, 튼튼한

It is big and strong. 그것은 크고 튼튼하다.
▶ having a lot of power or force; the opposite of weak

More 비교변화 strong - stronger - strongest

CHAPTER 1

UNIT 23 — Word 265~276

Shadow Speaking 332

듣기 046 말하기 047

265 **pocket** [pɔ́kit] 주머니
My pocket is full. 내 주머니가 가득하다.
▶ a small opening in or on a coat, pants, etc. where you can put money, keys, etc.

266 **bean** [biːn] 콩
The basket is full of beans. 그 바구니에 콩들이 가득하다.
▶ a seed or pod of a plant from the legume family

267 **but** [bʌt] 그러나
He is poor, but he is happy. 그는 가난 하지만 행복하다.
▶ used to join two sentences, word or groups of word to show a difference

More and 그리고, so 그래서, or 또는

268 **wind** [wind] 바람
The wind is warm. 바람이 따뜻하다.
▶ movement of air

269 **kind** [kaind] 친절한
He is kind to help me. 그는 나를 도와줘서 친절하다.
▶ warm and helpful; nice; friendly

More 비교변화 kind - kinder - kindest

270 **brown** [braun] 갈색(의)
She has brown eyes. 그녀가 갈색 눈을 가지고 있다.
▶ the color of chocolate or mud, etc.

UNIT 23

271 **snake** [sneik] 뱀

Snakes cannot walk. 뱀은 걷지 못한다.
▶a long animal that has a narrow body, scaly skin, and no arms or legs

272 **sweet** [swiːt] 달콤한

These cookies are sweet. 이 쿠키는 달콤하다.
▶tasting like sugar

More 비교변화 sweet - sweeter - sweetest, sweets 단것

273 **air** [ɛər] 공기

The air is fresh. 공기가 상쾌하다.
▶the mixture of gases on earth and that we breathe to live

274 **think** [θiŋk] 생각하다

I think the baby is cute. 나는 그 아기가 귀엽다고 생각한다.
▶to see or create something in your mind have as an opinion

More 동사변화 think - thought - thought, thought 생각

275 **field** [fiːld] 들판

The farmer grows oranges on the field.
농부가 들판에서 오렌지를 재배한다.
▶a piece of land that is used for growing plants

276 **mad** [mæd] 화난, 미친, 열광적인

What is he so mad about? 그는 무엇 때문에 그렇게 화내고 있니?
▶angry; crazy; liking someone or something very much

More 비교변화 mad - madder - maddest

CHAPTER 1

UNIT 24 — Word 277~288

Shadow Speaking 332

듣기 048 말하기 049

277 **act** [ækt] 행동하다
He acts like a child. 그는 어린이처럼 행동한다.
▶to behave; to do something

278 **great** [greit] 훌륭한
She does great work. 그녀는 훌륭한 일을 한다.
▶very good

More 비교변화 great - greater - greatest

279 **sleep** [sli:p] 잠, 잠자다
The baby is sleeping in this room.
그 아기가 이 방에서 잠을 자고 있다.
▶period when the mind rests and the body refreshes itself; to go to sleep

More 동사변화 sleep - slept - slept

280 **up** [ʌp] 위로
We went up the mountain. 우리는 산을 올라갔다.
▶toward the top

281 **shoe** [ʃu:] 신발, 구두
Put on your shoes. 신발을 신어라.
▶something that you wear on your feet for walking

282 **again** [əɡéin] 또, 다시
He tried it again. 그는 그것을 다시 시도했다.
▶once more; another time

UNIT 24

283 **every** [évri:] 모든

Every student passed the exam. 모든 학생들이 시험에 합격했다.
▶including each person or thing in a group
More each 각자, all 모두

284 **fruit** [fru:t] 과일

Grapes are my favorite fruit. 포도는 내가 가장 좋아하는 과일이다.
▶the part of a plant that has a seed and that can usually be aten, usually with a sweet taste

285 **bring** [briŋ] 가져오다

Bring me an eraser. 지우개를 가져와라.
▶to take something or somebody with oneself
More 동사변화 bring - brought - brought

286 **day** [dei] 하루, 낮

I studied all day. 나는 하루 종일 공부했다.
▶a period of 24 hours; the period of time between sunrise and sunset
More night 밤

287 **left** [left] 왼쪽(의)

Go to the left side. 왼쪽으로 가라.
▶the side or direction that is west of you when you face north
More right 오른쪽(의)

288 **jam** [dʒæm] 잼

You can make jam with strawberries. 너는 딸기로 잼을 만들 수 있다.
▶a thick paste that is made by cooking fruit with sugar

CHAPTER 1

UNIT 25

Word 289~300

Shadow Speaking 332

---

289 hand [hænd] 손

Wash your hands first. 먼저 너의 손을 씻어라
▶the part of the body containing fingers which is attached to the arm

---

290 seat [si:t] 좌석, 자리

Go back to your seat. 네 자리로 돌아가라.
▶something made to sit on

---

291 half [hæf] 절반, 반

Cut the watermelon in half. 그 수박을 반으로 잘라라.
▶one of two equal parts of something that make up a whole

More quarter 4분의 1, in half 반으로

---

292 supper [sʌ́pər] 저녁 식사

Don't eat much for supper. 저녁을 많이 먹지 마라.
▶a meal that is eaten in the evening dinner

More meal 식사, dinner 저녁 식사

---

293 belt [belt] 띠, 벨트

Fasten your seat belt. 좌석 벨트를 매라.
▶a strip of cloth or leather that is usually worn around the waist

---

294 dish [diʃ] 접시

Place the fruit on this dish. 이 접시에 그 과일을 놓아라.
▶an object on which food is served

UNIT 25

295 arrive [əráiv] 도착하다

We finally arrived at the station. 우리는 결국 역에 도착했다.
▶to reach a place

More arrival 도착

296 wash [wɑʃ] 씻다

I sometimes wash the dishes. 나는 때때로 설거지를 한다.
▶to make clean using water and soap

More wash[do] the dishes 설거지를 하다

297 pants [pænts] 바지

Put on your pants. 바지 입어라.
▶a piece of clothing that covers the each leg separately and the waist

More shorts 반바지, overalls 멜빵바지

298 paper [péipər] 종이

I need a pencil, an eraser and a piece of paper.
나는 연필과 지우개 그리고 종이가 필요하다.
▶a thin sheet usually made from wood that is used to write on, wrap things, cover walls, etc.

299 boat [bout] 보트, 작은 배

Row the boat. 보트를 저라.
▶something that floats and can carry a person over water

More ship 배, yacht 요트

300 start [stɑːrt] 시작하다

He and I started the computer games.
그와 나는 컴퓨터 게임을 시작했다.
▶to begin doing something; to go or put into action or motion

CHAPTER 1

UNIT 26

Word 301~312

Shadow Speaking 332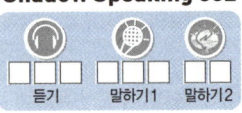

듣기 052 말하기 053

301 stamp [stæmp] 우표

I bought a stamp album in the stationery.
나는 문구점에서 우표첩을 샀다.
▶ a small piece of paper that you buy and then stick to an envelope or package to pay the cost of mailing it

302 talk [tɔ:k] 말하다

Don't talk so loud here. 여기서 그렇게 크게 말하지 마라.
▶ to say something

303 love [lʌv] 사랑, 사랑하다

I love mom and dad. 나는 엄마와 아빠를 사랑한다.
▶ a feeling of strong or constant affection for a person; to care for deeply and be devoted to

304 monkey [mʌ́ŋki] 원숭이

I went to the zoo and looked at the monkey.
나는 동물원에 가서 원숭이를 보았다.
▶ the kind of animal most similar to humans, with two arms, two legs and a tail

305 egg [eg] 달걀

I like boiled eggs. 나는 삶은 달걀을 좋아한다.
▶ a shell containing an unborn animal which is laid by birds

306 star [stɑ:r] 별

There are many stars in the sky. 하늘에 많은 별들이 있다.
▶ a ball of gas in the sky that shines

UNIT 26

307 morning [mɔ́ːrniŋ] 아침

I usually get up at six in the morning.
나는 보통 아침 6시에 일어난다.
▶ the time of the day when the sun is rising, around 6:00 am-11:59 am

308 try [trai] 노력하다

I try to do my best all the time. 나는 항상 최선을 다해 노력한다.
▶ to make an effort to do something

More try to ~하려고 노력하다, try on 입어보다

309 clean [kliːn] 깨끗한, 깨끗하게 하다

Today I cleaned my room. 오늘 나는 나의 방을 청소했다.
▶ pure; having no dirt; to remove the dirt from something

More 비교변화 clean - cleaner - cleanest

310 bowl [boul] 사발

I bought a plastic bowl yesterday. 나는 어제 플라스틱 사발을 샀다.
▶ a round deep dish

311 let [let] ~하게 하다

She let me know the truth. 그녀는 나에게 그 사실을 알려주었다.
▶ to allow someone to do something; to allow to happen

More 동사변화 let -let -let

312 often [ɔ́(ː)ftən] 종종, 자주

I often play with my little sister. 나는 여동생과 자주 논다.
▶ regularly; many times

More always 항상, usually 보통, sometimes 때때로, never 결코 ~ 아닌

CHAPTER 1

UNIT 27

Word 313~324

Shadow Speaking 332

듣기 054 말하기 055

313 soap [soup] 비누

Wash your hands with soap. 비누로 손을 씻어라.
▶ a kind of object or liquid used for cleaning

314 around [əràund] 주위에

The earth goes around the sun. 지구는 태양 주위를 돈다.
▶ at every side of something; in the area; nearby

315 look [luk] 보다

Look at the baby bear. 저 아기 곰 좀 봐.
▶ to turn your eyes toward something, so that you can see it

316 slow [slou] 느린

The turtle is slow. 그 거북은 느리다.
▶ moving at a low speed not fast

More 비교변화 slow - slower - slowest

317 farm [fɑːrm] 농장

My father has a farm. 나의 아버지는 농장을 가지고 계신다.
▶ a place where animals are raised or plants are grown for food

More farmer 농부, fish farm 양식장

318 ask [æsk] 질문하다

May I ask a question? 질문해도 될까요?
▶ to make a question about; to make a request

UNIT 27

319 pretty [príti] 예쁜

The girl is very pretty. 그 소녀는 매우 예쁘다.
▶attractive to look at usually in a graceful way; beautiful

More 비교변화 pretty - prettier - prettiest

320 window [wíndou] 창문

Look out of the window. 창 밖을 봐.
▶an opening in the wall of a building or vehicle that lets in light

321 grandfather [grǽndfɑ̀:ðər] 할아버지

My grandfather is very kind. 우리 할아버지는 매우 친절하시다.
▶the father of one's mother or father

More grandmother 할머니, grandparents 조부모님

322 glad [glæd] 기쁜

Glad to meet you. 만나서 기뻐.
▶feeling pleasure, joy, or delight

More 비교변화 glad - gladder - gladdest

323 office [ɔ́(:)fis] 사무실

Mr. Baker is working in this office.
Baker 씨는 이 사무실에서 일하고 있다.
▶a place where business is done

324 early [ə́:rli] 일찍

My brother and I wake up early in the morning.
형과 나는 아침에 일찍 일어난다.
▶near the beginning of a period of time

More 비교변화 early - earlier - earliest

CHAPTER 1

Word 325~336

Shadow Speaking 332

---

325 climb [klaim] 오르다, 올라가다

As they climbed higher, the air became cooler.
그들이 높이 올라갈수록 공기가 서늘해졌다.
▶to go up something by using one's body

326 evening [íːvniŋ] 저녁

My sister does her homework in the evening.
나의 언니는 저녁에 숙제를 한다.
▶the time of day following the afternoon and before midnight

327 dirty [dəːrti] 더러운

We clean up the dirty room. 우리는 더러운 방을 청소한다.
▶not clean; having dirt

More 비교변화 dirty - dirtier - dirtiest

328 uncle [ʌ́ŋkəl] 삼촌, 외삼촌

My uncle works at the bank. 나의 삼촌은 은행에서 일하신다.
▶father or mother's brother or brother-in-law

329 smile [smail] 웃다, 미소

I looked into the mirror and smiled.
나는 거울을 보고 웃었다.
▶to raise the ends of the lips to express happiness; the form of your lips when you smile

330 country [kʌ́ntri] 시골, 나라

She lives in the country. 그녀는 시골에서 산다.
▶the area outside of cities and towns; a nation

UNIT 28

331 **low** [lou] 낮은

This chair is too low for me. 이 의자는 내게 너무 낮다.
▶ of little distance from the ground; the opposite of high

More 비교변화 low - lower - lowest, high 높은

332 **niece** [niːs] 여자 조카

She lives with her niece. 그녀는 그녀의 조카딸과 함께 산다.
▶ a daughter of one's sister or brother

More nephew 남자 조카

333 **wing** [wiŋ] 날개

The birds have beautiful wings.
그 새들은 아름다운 날개를 가지고 있다.
▶ the part of a bird's body which allows it to fly

334 **thin** [θin] 얇은

This new book is thin. 이 새로운 책은 얇다.
▶ being small in width; slender

More 비교변화 thin - thinner - thinnest

335 **like** [laik] 좋아하다

I like apples and bananas. 나는 사과와 바나나를 좋아한다.
▶ to enjoy something or think that it is nice or good

336 **train** [trein] 기차

They are going to Busan by train. 그들은 기차로 부산에 가고 있다.
▶ a group of connected carriages that move on a railroad

CHAPTER 1

UNIT 29

Word 337~348

Shadow Speaking 332

듣기 058 말하기 059

337 sandwich [sǽndwitʃ] 샌드위치

I like cheese **sandwiches**. 나는 치즈 샌드위치를 좋아한다.
▶ a food that is made of two slices of bread with food between the slices

338 horse [hɔːrs] 말

I like to ride **horses**. 난 말 타는 것을 좋아한다.
▶ a kind of large strong animal that people ride and use for pulling heavy things

339 finger [fíŋɡər] 손가락

We have ten **fingers**. 우리는 손가락이 10개이다.
▶ one of the five thin parts of your hand

340 this [ðis] 이, 이것

This is a notebook. 이것은 공책이다.
▶ a word used to refer to something or someone nearby

341 doctor [dάktər] 의사

She is a **doctor**. 그녀는 의사이다.
▶ a person whose job it is to care for people's health
More dentist 치과 의사, nurse 간호사

342 house [haus] 집

My **house** is next to the library. 나의 집은 도서관 옆에 있다.
▶ a building that one or a few families live in

UNIT 29

343 **grandmother** [grǽndmʌ̀ðər] 할머니

I'll visit my grandmother in Busan.
나는 부산에 계신 할머니를 방문할 것이다.
▶the mother of one's mother or father

344 **high** [hai] 높은

The wall is very high. 그 벽은 매우 높다.
▶taller than usual; having a long length upward

More 비교변화 high - higher - highest, low 낮은

345 **meat** [miːt] 고기

The meat is really tough. 고기가 정말 질기다.
▶the flesh of a dead animal that can be eaten

More fish 생선, fruit 과일, vegetable 야채

346 **short** [ʃɔːrt] 짧은

The baby has short hair. 그 아기는 머리카락이 짧다.
▶having little length; the opposite of long

More 비교변화 short - shorter - shortest, long 긴

347 **never** [névər] 결코 ~하지 않은

I'll never forget your help. 나는 너의 도움을 결코 잊지 않을 것이다.
▶not at any time

More sometimes 때때로, often 종종, usually 보통, always 항상

348 **parents** [pέərənts] 부모님

My parents like to play badminton.
나의 부모님은 배드민턴 치는 것을 좋아하신다.
▶the mother and father of a child

CHAPTER 1

UNIT 30 — Word 349~360

Shadow Speaking 332

---

349 ball [bɔːl] 공

I bought a new soccer ball yesterday.
나는 어제 새 축구공을 샀다.
▶a round object used in games

350 water [wɔ́ːtər] 물

We cannot live without water. 우리는 물 없이 살 수 없다.
▶a clear liquid that has very little taste and is necessary for things to live

351 worker [wə́ːrkər] 노동자

His father is an office worker. 그의 아버지는 사무직 노동자이다.
▶a person who works

352 name [neim] 이름

What is your name? 너의 이름이 뭐니?
▶what a person, place, thing is called

353 store [stɔːr] 가게

I will go to the toy store. 나는 장난감 가게에 갈 것이다.
▶room or building where things are sold

More stationery store 문구점, department store 백화점, bookstore 서점

354 bull [bul] 황소

The bulls are grazing in the field.
그 황소들이 들판에서 풀을 뜯고 있다.
▶a male cow

UNIT 30

355 airplane [ɛ́ərplèin] 비행기
I will go there by airplane. 나는 비행기로 거기에 갈 것이다.
▶a vehicle with two wings that can fly in the air

356 tonight [tunáit] 오늘밤(에)
They have to say good-bye tonight.
그들은 오늘밤에 작별 인사를 해야 한다.
▶the present night

357 painter [péintər] 화가
Her mother is a famous painter. 그녀의 어머니는 유명한 화가이시다.
▶a person who paints

358 fat [fæt] 뚱뚱한
Chocolate can also make you fat.
초콜릿은 역시 당신을 뚱뚱하게 만들 수 있다.
▶having too much weight; having a lot of body fat

More 비교변화 fat - fatter - fattest

359 study [stʌ́di] 공부하다
She studied hard to pass the exam.
그녀는 시험에 합격하기 위해 열심히 공부했다.
▶to actively learn about a subject

360 read [riːd] 읽다
I read three books yesterday. 나는 어제 책 3권을 읽었다.
▶to look at the word of a book or other material to know what is written there

More 동사변화 read - read[red] - read[red]

CHAPTER 1

UNIT 31

Word 361~372

Shadow Speaking 332

듣기 062 말하기 063

361 lady [léidi] 숙녀

The lady is my aunt. 그 숙녀는 나의 이모이다.
▶polite word for a female adult woman

More gentleman 신사

362 sister [sístər] 여자형제, 언니, 여동생, 누나

She is my older sister. 그녀는 나의 언니이다.
▶a female that has the same parents as another

More brother 남자형제, 오빠, 형, 남동생

363 road [roud] 길

That road is very wide. 저 길은 매우 넓다.
▶a path on the ground that is made for people or other things to travel on

364 nurse [nə:rs] 간호사

My mother works at a hospital as a nurse.
나의 어머니는 병원에서 간호사로 일하신다.
▶a person who helps doctors take care of sick people

365 socks [sɑks] 양말

Where are my socks? 내 양말 어디에 있니?
▶coverings that are worn over the feet

366 home [houm] 집

We have to go home now. 우리는 지금 집에 가야 한다.
▶a place where one lives

UNIT 31

367 **soccer** [sάkər] 축구

Who is your favorite soccer player?
당신이 가장 좋아하는 축구 선수는 누구인가요?
▶ a game played with two teams, where a ball must be moved into a goal without using one's hands or arms

368 **dinner** [dínər] 정찬, 저녁 식사

Let's invite them to dinner tomorrow.
그들을 내일 저녁 식사에 초대하자.
▶ the main meal of the day; a meal that is eaten in the evening

369 **comb** [koum] 빗, 빗질하다

I comb my hair in the morning.
나는 아침에 빗으로 머리를 빗는다.
▶ a tool with stiff fork-like teeth used to style hair; to use a comb

370 **hobby** [hάbi] 취미

My hobby is collecting stamps. 나의 취미는 우표 수집이다.
▶ an activity that you regularly do for pleasure

371 **son** [sʌn] 아들

I have one son and two daughters. 나는 1남 2녀의 자녀를 두었다.
▶ a male child of a couple

More daughter 딸

372 **address** [ədrés] 주소

She asked for my email address. 그녀는 나의 이메일 주소를 물어봤다.
▶ a description of the location of a place that includes its city, street, and building number

CHAPTER 1

UNIT 32 — Word 373~384

Shadow Speaking 332

듣기 064 말하기 065

373 **lion** [láiən] 사자
I saw lions at the zoo last Sunday.
나는 지난 일요일에 동물원에서 사자를 보았다.
▶ a large, wild animal from the cat family with yellowish fur and a tail

374 **number** [nʌ́mbər] 숫자
My favorite number is three. 내가 가장 좋아하는 숫자는 3이다.
▶ a math symbol that shows a quantity

375 **stupid** [stjúːpid] 어리석은, 멍청한
It was a very stupid thing to do. 그것은 매우 어리석은 짓이었다.
▶ dumb; idiotic; not smart

More 비교변화 stupid - stupider - stupidest

376 **refrigerator** [rifrìdʒəréitər] 냉장고
Our refrigerator is out of order. 우리 냉장고는 고장이 났다.
▶ a device that keeps food cold and fresh

More out of order 고장이 난

377 **tomorrow** [tumɔ́ːrou] 내일
He is leaving tomorrow. 그는 내일 떠날 예정이다.
▶ the day after today

378 **ear** [iər] 귀
Rabbits have long ears. 토끼는 귀가 길다.
▶ the part of the head that is used to hear

UNIT 32

379 **paint** [peint] 페인트, 칠하다

I am painting the picture. 나는 그림을 색칠하고 있다.
▶a colored liquid mixture that is used to give color to objects; to make pictures using paint

380 **rich** [ritʃ] 부유한

He is very rich, but his brother is poor.
그는 매우 부유하지만 그의 동생은 가난하다.
▶having a lot of money; the opposite of poor

More 비교변화 rich - richer - richest, poor 가난한

381 **cover** [kʌ́vər] 표지, 덮다

The storybook has a blue cover. 그 이야기책은 표지가 파란색이다.
▶the outer paper or board over the pages of a book; to put something over something else

382 **quick** [kwik] 빠른

Leopards are quick animals. 표범은 빠른 동물이다.
▶going at a high speed

More 비교변화 quick - quicker - quickest, slow 느린

383 **expensive** [ikspénsiv] 비싼

Her bag is very expensive. 그녀의 가방은 매우 비싸다.
▶costing a lot of money; the opposite of cheap

More 비교변화 expensive - more expensive - most expensive, cheap 싼

384 **hair** [hɛər] 머리카락

My mother has long hair. 나의 어머니는 머리카락이 길다.
▶a thread like form that grows outward from under the skin

CHAPTER 1

UNIT 33

Word 385~396

듣기 066 말하기 067

385 movie [múːvi] 영화

Do you plan to see the movie? 너는 그 영화를 볼 계획이니?
▶ a motion picture

386 neck [nek] 목

Giraffes have long necks. 기린은 목이 길다.
▶ the part of the body between the head and shoulders

387 eat [iːt] 먹다

We eat turkey on Thanksgiving.
우리는 추수 감사절에 칠면조 고기를 먹는다.
▶ to put food into one's mouth, then chew and swallow it

More 동사변화 eat - ate - eaten

388 yellow [jélou] 노란색

I like that yellow toy car. 나는 저 노란색 장난감 차가 좋다.
▶ the color of the sun or butter, etc.

389 jacket [dʒǽkit] 재킷

I like the black jacket. 난 검정색 재킷이 맘에 든다.
▶ a piece of clothing that covers the arms and trunk or more of the body

390 way [wei] 길, 방법

Where there is a will, there is a way.
뜻이 있는 곳에 길이 있다.
▶ course; how something is done

UNIT 33

391 month [mʌnθ] 달, 개월

January is the first month of the year.
1월은 1년 중에 첫 번째 달이다.
▶ one of twelve divisions of a year

More year 년, day 일, week 주

392 nephew [néfju:] 남자 조카

I played soccer with my nephew last Monday.
나는 지난 월요일에 조카와 축구를 했다.
▶ the son of one's sisters or brothers

More niece 여자 조카

393 letter [létər] 편지, 글자

I got a letter yesterday. 나는 어제 편지를 받았다.
▶ a written message that is sent to someone; a symbol that represents a sound from a language

394 wide [waid] 넓은

The river is wide and deep. 그 강은 넓고 깊다.
▶ large from side to side

More 비교변화 wide - wider - widest, width 폭, 너비

395 animal [ǽnəməl] 동물

A dolphin is an animal. 돌고래는 동물이다.
▶ a living thing that is not a plant, person

More insect 곤충, fish 어류, bird 조류

396 dry [drai] 마른

Your clothes and pants are dry. 너의 옷과 바지가 말랐다.
▶ having no moisture; the opposite of wet

More 비교변화 dry - drier - driest, wet 젖은

CHAPTER 1

UNIT 34
Word 397~408

Shadow Speaking 332

듣기 068 말하기 069

397 spoon [spuːn] 숟가락

Eat soup with a spoon. 숟가락으로 수프를 먹어라.
▶ a tool that has a handle and a small bowl and is used for eating or cooking

More fork 포크, chopsticks 젓가락

398 far [fɑːr] 멀리

Our school is far from my house. 우리 학교는 나의 집에서 멀다
▶ a long distance from

399 boot [buːt] 장화

Put on your boots. 장화를 신어라.
▶ a shoe that covers the foot and part of the leg

400 hate [heit] 싫어하다

I hate snakes. 나는 뱀이 싫다.
▶ to strongly dislike someone or something

401 dance [dæns] 춤추다

I can sing and dance. 나는 노래를 부르고 춤을 출 수 있다.
▶ to move along with music

402 learn [ləːrn] 배우다

I want to learn about birds and animals.
나는 새와 동물에 대해 배우고 싶다.
▶ to gain knowledge of something through study, instruction or experience

76 · Shadow Speaking 332

UNIT 34

403 as [æz] ~할 때, ~만큼, ~로, ~으로써

I saw a snake as I was going to the market.
나는 시장에 가면서 뱀을 봤다.
▶ at the same time; in the state of; in the quality of

404 deep [di:p] 깊은

The hole is very deep. 이 구멍은 매우 깊다.
▶ having a long distance downward

More 비교변화 deep - deeper - deepest, depth 깊이

405 world [wə:rld] 세계

She traveled around the world. 그녀는 세계 곳곳을 여행했다.
▶ the earth and all the people and everything on it

406 before [bifɔ:r] ~ 전에(시간), ~ 앞에(장소)

Wash your hands before you eat. 식사하기 전에 손 씻어라.
▶ at an earlier time; in front of something

More after ~ 후에, during ~ 동안

407 mail [meil] 우편, 우편물

I got a lot of mail yesterday. 나는 어제 우편물을 많이 받았다.
▶ something that is sent or carried by a delivery service

More email 이메일(전자우편), mailman 우편배달부

408 pick [pik] 꺾다, 고르다

I picked a white rose. 나는 하얀 빨간 장미 한 송이를 꺾었다.
▶ to remove a flower, fruit, nut etc. from a plant or tree; to choose a person or thingt

More pick up 줍다

CHAPTER 1

UNIT 35

Word 409~420

듣기 070 말하기 071

409 music [mjúːzik] 음악

Last Sunday I stayed home and listened to music.
지난 일요일에 나는 집에 있으면서 음악 들었다.
▶rhythmic sounds made by singing or playing an instrument.

410 grow [grou] 자라다

A tadpole grows into a frog. 올챙이는 자라서 개구리가 된다.
▶to have one's body develop over time

411 much [mʌtʃ] (양이) 많은

I ate too much. 나는 너무 많이 먹었다.
▶a large amount of; a lot of, used with uncountable nouns

More 비교변화 much - more - most, many (수가) 많은

412 helicopter [hélikɔ̀ptər] 헬리콥터

I bought him a toy helicopter. 나는 그에게 장난감 헬리콥터를 사줬다.
▶a vehicle that has long horizontal blades on top that spin, enabling it to fly in the air

413 bell [bel] 종

The bell is ringing. 그 종이 울리고 있다.
▶an instrument that is shaken to make a ringing sound

414 off [ɔːf] ~에서 벗어나

We take off our shoes in the house. 우리는 집에서 신발을 벗는다.
▶so as to be removed

UNIT 35

415 north [nɔːrθ] 북쪽

Let's go to the north. 북쪽으로 가자.
▶the direction that is left of the sunrise

416 just [dʒʌst] 단지, 금방

I'm just watching TV. 나는 단지 TV를 보고 있다.
▶only; a short time before

417 frog [frɔːg] 개구리

The frog is jumping into the pond now.
그 개구리가 지금 연못으로 뛰고 있다.
▶an animal that lives near water with smooth skin, big eyes, four legs, and webbed feet for swimming and jumping

418 bat [bæt] 야구 방망이, 박쥐

Bats live in the cave. 박쥐는 동굴에서 산다.
▶a thick stick for hitting a ball in baseball; an animal that looks like a mouse with wings and lives in a cave

419 cheap [tʃiːp] 값이 싼

I know a very cheap store. 나는 값이 싼 가게를 알고 있다.
▶having a low price

More 비교변화 cheap - cheaper - cheapest, expensive 비싼

420 pig [pig] 돼지

I have five pigs. 나는 돼지 5마리를 가지고 있다.
▶a farm animal with short legs, a fat body, and a curved tail that is raised for its meat

CHAPTER 1

UNIT 36

Word 421~432

Shadow Speaking 332

듣기 072 말하기 073

421 pear [pɛər] (과일) 배

I like pears best. 나는 배를 가장 좋아한다.
▶a kind of sweet juicy fruit with a thin skin

422 ago [əgóu] 전에

He and she came to Paris three years ago.
그와 그녀는 3년 전에 파리로 왔다.
▶in the past; before

423 cloud [klaud] 구름

The mountain is covered with clouds. 그 산은 구름에 덮여 있다.
▶a gray or white body floating in the sky that create rain

424 long [lɔːŋ] 긴

We have a long vacation. 우리에게는 긴 방학이 있다.
▶having a large length or duration

More 비교변화 long - longer - longest, short 짧은

425 skirt [skəːrt] 치마

She is wearing a blue skirt and a white sweater.
그녀는 파란색 치마와 흰색 스웨터를 입고 있다.
▶a piece of clothing which hangs down from the waist like the bottom part of a dress

426 mirror [mírər] 거울

The girl looks into the mirror. 그 소녀는 거울을 본다.
▶a smooth or polished surface that reflects images

UNIT 36

427 right [rait] 오른쪽(의), 올바른

Go straight and turn right at the police station.
직진한 후에 경찰서에서 우회전해라.
▶ the side or direction that is east of you when you face north; correct and proper

More left 왼쪽(의)

428 sea [siː] 바다

I can swim in the sea. 나는 바다에서 수영할 수 있다.
▶ salt water that is smaller than an ocean

429 by [bai] ~ 옆에

There is the toy car by the soccer ball.
그 축구공 옆에 그 장난감 차가 있다.
▶ next to; close to

430 class [klæs] 반, 수업

We have English class today. 우리 오늘 영어 수업 있다.
▶ a group of students meeting regularly to study; the period during which such a group meets

431 candle [kǽndl] 양초

We lighted a candle. 우리는 양초를 켰다.
▶ a wax stick with a string that comes out at the top that is burned to create light

432 goat [gout] 염소

The goat is crying in the grass. 염소가 풀밭에서 울고 있다.
▶ a sheep-like animal with two horns and usually straight hair which is raised for its milk, meat, and hair

CHAPTER 1

UNIT 37

Word 433~444

Shadow Speaking 332

듣기 074 말하기 075

433 **floor** [flɔːr] 바닥, 층

My classroom is on the second floor. 나의 교실은 2층에 있다.
▶the bottom surface of a room; a level of a building

434 **idea** [aidíːə] 생각

I have a good idea. 나는 좋은 생각이 있다.
▶a thought or picture created by the mind

435 **lesson** [lésn] 수업

I have a piano lesson this afternoon.
나는 오늘 오후에 피아노 수업이 있다.
▶a period of time when something is taught; something that is learned

436 **family** [fǽməli] 가족

I play tennis with my family every Sunday.
나는 매주 일요일에 가족과 테니스를 친다.
▶a group of people that includes parents and their children

437 **chin** [tʃin] 턱

He hurt his chin. 그는 턱을 다쳤다.
▶the lower part of one's face below one's lips

438 **sick** [sik] 아픈

I was sick yesterday. 나는 어제 아팠다.
▶not feeling well; ill

More 비교변화 sick - sicker - sickest

UNIT 37

439 say [sei] 말하다

He said, "She is kind." "그녀는 친절해."라고 그가 말했어
▶ to use your voice to express with word

More 동사변화 say - said - said

440 visit [vízit] 방문하다

I visited my grandparents on vacation.
나는 방학에 조부모님 댁을 방문했다.
▶ to go to see someone or some place

More 동사변화 visit - visited - visited

441 year [jiər] 해, 년

He visited Paris last year. 그는 작년에 파리를 방문했다.
▶ a length of time that is 365 days

More day 하루, month 월, day of week 요일

442 check [tʃek] 점검하다, 조사하다

Go and check your accounts. 가서 너의 계산서를 점검해라.
▶ to look over something to see whether it is correct

443 rain [rein] 비, 비가 오다

It will rain tomorrow. 내일 비가 올 것이다.
▶ drops of water that fall from the clouds; to fall in drops of water

444 or [ɔːr] 또는

Which do you like better, soccer or baseball?
너는 축구와 야구 중에 어느 것을 더 좋아하니?
▶ a word used to show more than one choice

CHAPTER 1

UNIT 38 — Word 445~456

Shadow Speaking 332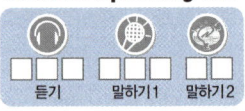

듣기 076 말하기 077

445 pencil [pénsəl] 연필

The boy gave the girl two pencils.
그 소년은 그 소녀에게 연필 2자루를 주었다.
▶a writing tool with graphite in the middleg

446 follow [fálou] 따르다

The child followed his mom into the house..
그 어린이는 그의 엄마를 따라 집으로 들어갔다.
▶to come or go after someone or something

447 jump [dʒʌmp] 뛰다, 뛰어오르다

She jumps forward three times. 그녀는 앞으로 3번 뛴다.
▶to spring into the air by pushing with your legs

448 nose [nouz] 코

Please touch your nose. 코를 만지세요.
▶the part of the face that is used for smelling or breathing

449 ant [ænt] 개미

Ants like sweet food. 개미들은 단 음식을 좋아한다.
▶a kind of small insect that lives in large groups

450 cut [kʌt] 베다, 자르다

She cut an apple in half. 그녀는 사과를 반으로 잘랐다.
▶to divide something with a knife, scissors, etc.

More 동사변화 cut - cut - cut

84 · Shadow Speaking 332

UNIT 38

451 **magic** [mǽdʒik] 마술, 마력

I don't believe in magic. 나는 마술을 믿지 않는다.
▶ an art that uses tricks an special powers

452 **seller** [sélər] 파는 사람, 판매자

I talked with the book seller yesterday.
나는 어제 책 판매원과 이야기를 했었다.
▶ a person who sells

More sell 팔다, buy 사다, buyer 구매자

453 **table** [téibəl] 탁자

There is a baseball glove under the table.
야구 글러브는 그 탁자 아래에 있다.
▶ a piece of furniture consisting of a flat board on legs

454 **rectangle** [réktæŋɡəl] 직사각형

He draws a rectangle in his notebook.
그는 그의 공책에 직사각형을 하나 그린다.
▶ a closed form that includes four straight sides and four right angles

More circle 원, triangle 삼각형, square 정사각형

455 **stand** [stænd] 서다

Please stand up and come here. 일어서서 이리로 오세요.
▶ to support oneself on one's feet while being in a straight position

More 동사변화 stand - stood - stood

456 **mother** [mʌ́ðər] 어머니

My mother is home now. 나의 어머니는 지금 집에 계신다.
▶ a female parent mom

CHAPTER 1

UNIT 39 Word 457~468

Shadow Speaking 332

듣기 078 말하기 079

457 door [dɔ:r] 문

Open the door, please. 문 좀 열어 주세요.
▶a flat board that can be moved to open and close an entrance

458 close [klouz] 닫다

Close your eyes. 눈을 감아라.
▶to move so that things cannot pass through an opening

459 here [hiər] 여기에

She put her bag here yesterday.
그녀는 그녀의 가방을 어제 여기에 놓았다.
▶in this place; in this location

460 moon [mu:n] 달

We looked at the moon through the telescope.
우리는 망원경으로 달을 보았다.
▶a natural object that rotates around a planet

461 listen [lísən] 듣다

My sister listens to rock music. 나의 누나는 락 음악을 듣는다.
▶to pay attention to sound

462 sunflower [sʌ́nflàuər] 해바라기

The girl is wearing a sunflower in her hair.
그 소녀는 머리에 해바라기를 달고 있다.
▶a flower with a large yellow head and seeds that people can eat

UNIT 39

463 catch [kætʃ] 잡다

He catches the ball. 그는 그 공을 잡는다.
▶to use your hands to grasp and hold

More 동사변화 catch - caught - caught

464 flag [flæg] 깃발

Hold your flag up, please. 깃발을 들어 주세요.
▶a piece of cloth that is attached to a pole and is used to represent a country or group, etc.

465 sit [sit] 앉다

The teacher sits on the chair. 그 선생님이 의자 위에 앉았다.
▶to rest on one's bottom such as in a chair or on a sofa

More 동사변화 sit - sit - sit

466 draw [drɔː] 그리다

I drew many flowers. 나는 많은 꽃들을 그렸다.
▶to make a picture using a pen, pencil, etc.

More 동사변화 draw - drew - drawn

467 foot [fut] 발

Please show me your right foot. 너의 오른쪽 발을 보여 주세요.
▶the part of the leg below the ankle that is used for standing and walking

More 복수형 feet

468 brother [brʌ́ðər] 남자 형제, 오빠, 형, 남동생

My older brother is very short. 우리 오빠는 키가 아주 작다.
▶a male sibling; the opposite of sister

More sister 여자형제, 언니, 누나, 여동생

CHAPTER 1

UNIT 40
Word 469~480

---

469 monster [mɑ́nstər] 괴물

He grew into a monster in the movie.
그는 영화에서 괴물로 변했다.
▶ a fake human or animal-like creature that is usually scary

470 pass [pæs] 건네주다, 통과하다

Would you pass me the eraser? 지우개 좀 건네줄래?
▶ to hand something to someone; to move past someone or something

471 stair [stɛər] 계단

Watch out for the stairs. 계단을 조심해라.
▶ a set of steps between two or more floors

472 show [ʃou] 보여주다, 알려주다

She showed me her new hat.
그녀는 나에게 그녀의 새 모자를 보여줬다.
▶ to let someone see something; to make something visible

More 동사변화 show - showed - showed/shown

473 question [kwéstʃən] 질문

That's a good question! 좋은 질문이다.
▶ something that you ask someone

474 corner [kɔ́:rnər] 구석, 모퉁이

Turn right at the corner. 모퉁이에서 오른쪽으로 돌아요.
▶ a place where lines meet

UNIT 40

475 **open** [óupən] 열다

Open your book to page 24. 책의 24쪽을 펴라.
▶to make the inside visible; the opposite of close

476 **wrong** [rɔːŋ] 잘못된, 틀린

If your partner is wrong, help him. 짝이 틀렸으면 도와줘라.
▶not correct; the opposite of right

More right 옳은, 맞은

477 **give** [giv] 주다

Give me some salt, please. 나에게 소금을 좀 주세요
▶to provide something to someone

More 동사변화 give - gave - given

478 **dining room** [dáiniŋrùːm] 식당, 주방

There was a knock at the dining room door suddenly.
갑자기 식당 문을 두드리는 소리가 났다.
▶a room in which people eat

479 **shoulder** [ʃóuldər] 어깨

Please point to your right shoulder. 오른쪽 어깨를 가리키세요.
▶the part of the body where the arm joins the trunk

More head 머리, knee 무릎, foot 발

480 **swim** [swim] 수영하다

I like to swim in the pool. 나는 수영장에 수영하는 것을 좋아한다.
▶to move yourself through water using your arms and legs; to move around in water

More 동사변화 swim - swam - swum

CHAPTER 1

UNIT 41 — Word 481~492

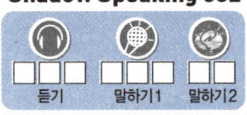

듣기 082 말하기 083

481 street [striːt] 거리, 길거리
I met a friend on the street. 나는 친구를 길거리에서 만났다.
▶ a road in a city or town where cars are able to travel

482 finish [fíniʃ] 끝내다
I finished my homework. 나는 숙제를 끝냈다.
▶ to stop doing; to bring to an end

483 purple [pə́ːrpəl] 자줏빛(의)
I would like a purple skirt. 나는 자주색 치마를 갖고 싶다.
▶ the color of grapes or lilies, etc.

484 buy [bai] 사다
I want to buy some flowers. 나는 약간의 꽃을 사고 싶다.
▶ to give money to get something
More 동사변화 buy - bought - bought

485 alone [əlóun] 혼자
I will be alone at home tomorrow. 나는 내일 집에 혼자 있을 것이다.
▶ by oneself; without anyone or anything

486 point [pɔint] 가리키다
My teacher pointed to the window. 나의 선생님은 그 창문을 가리키셨다.
▶ to indicate something with a finger, hand or object

UNIT 41

487 **gray** [grei] 회색(의)

He is wearing a gray hat. 그는 회색 모자를 쓰고 있다.
▶the color which is a mix of black and white

488 **kitchen** [kítʃən] 부엌

My father is cooking in the kitchen.
나의 아버지는 부엌에서 요리를 하시고 계신다.
▶a room used for cooking

489 **behind** [biháind] ~ 뒤에

The stationery is behind the post office.
그 문구점은 우체국 뒤에 있다.
▶coming after in place, time, or order
More in front of ~ 앞에

490 **down** [daun] 아래로(에)

People climbed down the mountain. 사람들은 그 산을 내려왔다.
▶the direction toward the ground
More up 위로(에)

491 **head** [hed] 머리

The bird is on my head. 그 새는 내 머리 위에 있다.
▶the part of the body with the brain, eyes, ears and mouth

492 **between** [bitwíːn] ~ 사이에(둘)

It's between the bank and the hospital.
그것은 은행과 병원 사이에 있다.
▶in the area that separates
More among ~ 중에, ~ 사이에(셋 이상)

CHAPTER 1

UNIT 42

Word 493~504

---

493 town [taun] 시내, 읍

I sometimes went to the town.
나는 때때로 시내에 갔었다.
▶an area where people live in with a place-name and smaller than a city

494 well [wel] 건강한, 잘

She plays the piano well. 그녀는 피아노를 잘 친다.
▶healthy; with skill; in a good manner

More 비교변화 well - better - best

495 invitation [ìnvətéiʃən] 초대

They made invitation cards. 그들은 초대 카드를 만들었다.
▶a request to attend something

More invite 초대하다

496 garden [gáːrdn] 정원

The garden is beautiful. 그 정원은 아름답다.
▶a place where people grow flowers or plants

497 lay [lei] 놓다, 두다

She laid the baby down on the bed. 그녀는 아기를 침대에 내려놓았다.
▶to place down gently in a flat position

More 동사변화 lay - laid - laid

498 car [kɑːr] 자동차

I went to the station by car. 나는 역까지 자동차로 갔다.
▶a vehicle with an engine and usually four wheels

UNIT 42

499 safe [seif] 안전한

This pool is safe. 이 수영장은 안전하다.
▶free from danger; the opposite of dangerous

More 비교변화 safe - safer - safest, dangerous 위험한, safety 안전

500 meet [miːt] 만나다

I met my teacher in the park. 나는 공원에서 나의 선생님을 만났다.
▶to come across a person; get to know a person; to get together with a person

More 동사변화 meet - met - met

501 thick [θik] 두꺼운

This book is too thick. 이 책은 너무 두껍다.
▶being large in width

More 비교변화 thick - thicker - thickest, thin 얇은

502 and [ænd] 그리고

It's sunny and hot. 화창하고 덥다.
▶used to join two sentences, word or groups of word to show similarity

503 night [nait] 밤

It is dark at night. 밤에는 어둡다.
▶the part of the day when there is no light

504 blanket [blǽŋkit] 담요

Her blanket is clean. 그녀의 담요는 깨끗하다.
▶a cloth covering that is used to keep the body warm as it sleeps

CHAPTER 1

UNIT 43

Word 505~516

Shadow Speaking 332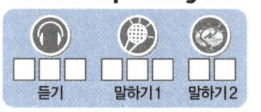

---

505 **dark** [dɑːrk] 어두운

It's dark in the cave. 동굴 안은 어둡다.
▶having little or no light

More 비교변화 dark - darker - darkest

506 **another** [ənʌ́ðər] 다른, 또 하나

Let's go to another place. 다른 장소로 가자.
▶some other; an additional

507 **out** [aut] 밖으로

Please let me go out. 나가게 해 주세요.
▶away from the inside

508 **cute** [kjuːt] 귀여운

My little sister is cute. 나의 여동생은 귀엽다.
▶looking beautiful in a sweet way

More 비교변화 cute - cuter - cutest

509 **move** [muːv] 움직이다, 이사하다

We moved into a new house. 우리는 새로운 집으로 이사했다.
▶to change position; to make something change position

510 **noon** [nuːn] 정오

Let's meet at noon in front of the museum.
박물관 앞에서 정오에 만나자.
▶12 o'clock in the middle of the day

UNIT 43

511　good [gud] 좋은

It's a good car in my town. 그것은 우리 마을에서 좋은 차이다.
▶kind; of high quality; the opposite of bad

More 비교변화 good - better - best

512　make [meik] 만들다

My brother and I made a snowman.
나의 남동생과 나는 눈사람을 만들었다.
▶to build, create, or produce something

More 동사변화 make - made - made

513　story [stɔ́ːri] 이야기

It is a story about good men. 그것은 좋은 사람들에 대한 이야기이다.
▶a description of something which tells about an event

514　triangle [tráiæŋɡəl] 삼각형, 트라이앵글

They are making a triangle. 그들은 삼각형을 만들고 있다.
▶a shape with three sides and whose angles add up to 180 degrees

515　song [sɔ(ː)ŋ] 노래

People dance and sing a song on the stage.
사람들이 무대에서 춤을 추며 노래를 부르고 있다.
▶a piece of music or the Word set to that piece

More sing 노래하다, singer 가수

516　then [ðen] 그때에

See you then. 그때 보자.
▶at that time or in that case

CHAPTER 1

UNIT 44

Word 517~528

듣기 088 말하기 089

517 once [wʌns] 한 번

The earth goes round the sun once a year.
지구는 1년에 한 번 태양 주위를 돈다.
▶one time only

518 pearl [pəːrl] 진주

She was wearing a pearl necklace. 그녀는 진주 목걸이를 하고 있었다.
▶a smooth, round stone made by clams and oysters

519 sing [siŋ] 노래하다

My sister sings a song well. 나의 언니는 노래를 잘 한다.
▶to make music with one's voice

More 동사변화 sing - sang - sung

520 together [təgéðər] 함께

They will play soccer together. 그들은 함께 축구를 할 것이다.
▶with another person or persons or in one place

521 use [juːs] 사용하다, 이용하다

Let's use the dictionary. 사전을 이용하자.
▶to do something with an object to get something done

522 quiet [kwáiət] 조용한

Be quiet in the museum, please. 박물관에서는 조용히 하세요.
▶having little or no sound; without much noise

More 비교변화 quiet - quieter - quietest

UNIT 44

523 **land** [lænd] 땅, 착륙하다

The US has lots of land. 미국은 넓은 땅을 가졌다.
▶any particular area of ground; to return to the ground (airplanes, ships)

More take off 이륙하다

524 **tennis** [ténis] 테니스

She plays tennis very well. 그녀는 테니스를 너무 잘 친다.
▶a game that is played with rackets and a light ball by two or more players on a court with a low net in the middle

525 **knee** [niː] 무릎

My knees hurt. 나는 무릎이 아프다.
▶the part in the middle of the leg, where the leg bends

526 **breakfast** [brékfəst] 아침 식사

I have breakfast at 8 o'clock. 나는 정각 8시에 아침 식사를 한다.
▶a meal eaten in the morning

More lunch 점심 식사, dinner 저녁 식사

527 **must** [mʌst] ~해야 한다

I must go home now. 나는 지금 집에 가야 한다.
▶used to say that something is required; have to

More must not ~해서는 안 된다(금지), don't have to ~할 필요가 없다(불필요)

528 **rabbit** [rǽbit] 토끼

I feed the rabbit every morning. 나는 매일 아침에 토끼 먹이를 준다.
▶a furry animal with two long ears, short tails, and long back legs

CHAPTER 1

UNIT 45

Word 529~540

Shadow Speaking 332

듣기 090 말하기 091

529 stay [stei] 머무르다

She will stay home all day long.
그녀는 하루 종일 집에 머물러 있을 것이다.
▶to continue to be in the same place for a period of time

530 until [əntíl] ~까지(시간)

I have to work until five. 나는 5시까지 일해야 한다.
▶up to the time that

531 hundred [hʌ́ndrəd] 100(백)

There are one hundred people in the building.
그 건물에는 100명의 사람들이 있다.
▶being ten more than ninety

More ten 10, thousand 1,000, million 100만

532 need [niːd] 필요하다

I need a new bike. 나는 새 자전거가 필요하다.
▶to be in a condition in which you must have something

533 thousand [θáuzənd] 1,000(천)

The T-shirt is five thousand won. 그 T셔츠는 5천 원이다.
▶the word for 1,000

534 live [liv] 살다

I live in Seoul. 나는 서울에 산다.
▶to be alive; to have a home

UNIT 45

535 vegetable [védʒətəbəl] 채소, 야채

I like fresh vegetables. 나는 싱싱한 야채를 좋아한다.
▶a plant that can be eaten that is not a fruit or seed

536 hard [hɑːrd] 딱딱한, 어려운

This ball is so hard. 이 공은 매우 딱딱하다.
▶not soft; difficult to do or understand; in an extreme manner

More 비교변화 hard - harder - hardest

537 airport [ɛ́ərpɔ̀ːrt] 공항

He works at the airport. 그는 공항에서 일한다.
▶a place where aircraft can take off and land

More port 항구, airline 항공사

538 poor [puər] 가난한, 불쌍한

The man is very poor. 그 남자는 매우 가난하다.
▶having little or no money; the opposite of rich

More 비교변화 poor - poorer - poorest, rich 부유한

539 begin [bigín] 시작하다

The school begins at nine. 그 학교는 9시에 시작한다.
▶to start doing something

More 동사변화 begin - began - begun, end 끝나다

540 warm [wɔːrm] 따뜻한

It's nice and warm. 날씨가 맑고 따뜻하다.
▶heated at a comfortable level

More 비교변화 warm - warmer - warmest

CHAPTER 1

UNIT 46

Word 541~552

---

541 **milk** [milk] 우유

Do you want some milk? 우유 좀 마실래?
▶a white liquid that is drunk by people and animals

542 **will** [wil] ~할 것이다

What will you do this summer? 너는 이번 여름에 뭐 할 거니?
▶a word expressing the future
More be going to ~할 것이다

543 **where** [hwɛər] 어디에

Where's my watch? 내 손목시계 어디 있니?
▶used to ask about a place something occurs

544 **candy** [kǽndi] 사탕

The children like cookies and candies.
어린이들은 쿠키와 사탕을 좋아한다
▶a sweet food made of mainly sugar

545 **ride** [raid] 타다

I like to ride a bike. 나는 자전거 타는 것을 좋아한다.
▶to sit or stand on top of an object while it is moving
More 동사변화 ride - rode - ridden

546 **any** [éni] 좀, 약간의

Do you have any pencils? 너는 연필 좀 있니?
▶some amount

UNIT 46

547 want [wɔ(:)nt] 원하다, ~하고 싶다

Do you want to sing now? 너는 지금 노래 부르고 싶니?
▶to desire to have or do something

548 side [said] 편

Which side are you on? 너는 어느 편이니?
▶one of two or more people or groups that are working or competing against each other

549 million [míljən] 100만

More than one million people live in Suwon.
100만 명이 넘는 사람들이 수원에 살고 있다.
▶the word for 1,000,000

More more than … 이상으로, 넘는

550 cool [ku:l] 시원한

Our classroom is cool. 우리 교실은 시원하다.
▶slightly cold; not warm or hot

More 비교변화 cool - cooler - coolest

551 tell [tel] 말하다

He told me funny stories. 그는 나에게 재미있는 이야기들을 말해 줬다.
▶to say something to someone

More 동사변화 tell - told - told

552 dolphin [dálfin] 돌고래

I saw the dolphin show at the zoo.
나는 동물원에서 돌고래 쇼를 봤다.
▶a very smart sea animal like a fish with a long gray pointed nose

CHAPTER 1

UNIT 47 — Word 553~564

Shadow Speaking 332

듣기 094 말하기 095

553 **hospital** [háspitl] 병원
I went to the hospital yesterday. 나는 어제 병원에 갔다.
▶a place where doctors and nurses help sick people

554 **come** [kʌm] 오다
He came to my house. 그는 나의 집에 왔다.
▶to move toward someone or something
More 동사변화 come - came - come

555 **word** [wəːrd] 단어, 말
I read this difficult word. 나는 이 어려운 단어를 읽는다.
▶the smallest part of a language that can be used on its own to convey meaning or function

556 **drink** [driŋk] 마시다
He is drinking water. 그는 물을 마시고 있다.
▶to take in a liquid through the mouth and swallow it
More 동사변화 drink - drank - drunk

557 **when** [hwen] 언제
When is your birthday? 너의 생일은 언제니?
▶at what time; at or during which time

558 **food** [fuːd] 음식
My favorite food is pizza. 내가 가장 좋아하는 음식은 피자이다.
▶something which is eaten and is necessary for life

UNIT 47

559 season [síːzən] 계절

What season do you like? 너는 어느 계절을 좋아하니?
▶ any of the four periods of the year that brings their own weather changes

More: spring 봄, summer 여름, fall 가을, winter 겨울

560 fall [fɔːl] 가을, 떨어지다

The rain fell down to the ground. 비가 땅으로 떨어졌다.
▶ the season between summer and winter; to drop down from a high place

More: 동사변화 fall - fell - fallen

561 what [hwɑt] 무엇

What do you want? 너는 무엇을 원하니?
▶ used to ask for information or for someone's opinion

562 do [duː] 하다

I do my homework every evening. 나는 숙제를 매일 저녁에 한다.
▶ to perform an action or activity

More: 동사변화 do - did - done

563 potato [pətéitou] 감자

I will wash these potatoes. 나는 이 감자들을 씻을 것이다.
▶ a round, starchy vegetable with a thin, paper-like skin

More: sweet potato 고구마

564 hold [hould] 갖고 있다, 잡다

Will you hold the bag? 그 가방 좀 들고 있을래?
▶ to perform have or keep something in your hands or arms

More: 동사변화 hold - held - held

CHAPTER 1

UNIT 48

Word 565~576

Shadow Speaking 332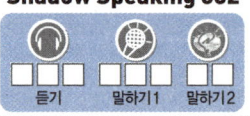

듣기 096 말하기 097

565 person [pə́ːrsən] 사람

She will be a great person. 그녀는 위대한 사람이 될 것이다.
▶a human; a human being

More 사람들 persons, people

566 shout [ʃaut] 소리치다

My brother is shouting at me. 나의 형이 나에게 소리치고 있다.
▶to make loud sounds with one's voice

567 across [əkrɔ́ːs] ~의 건너편의

The girl is across the street. 그 소녀는 길 건너편에 있다.
▶on the opposite side of; to the other side of

568 problem [prɑ́bləm] 문제

This is not a difficult problem to solve.
이것은 풀기에 어려운 문제가 아니다.
▶something that is difficult to deal with

569 past [pæst] 과거

I often went there with my mother in the past.
나는 과거에 나의 어머니와 함께 거기에 자주 갔었다.
▶the time before the present

570 true [truː] 진실의, 사실의

Is it true? 그것이 사실이니?
▶real; accurate; the opposite of false

More 비교변화 true - truer - truest

UNIT 48

571 **how** [hau] 어떻게

How did you get there? 너는 거기에 어떻게 갔니?
▶in what way; in what amount or size

More how many 얼마나 많은, how old 얼마나 오래, how often 얼마나 자주, how far 얼마나 멀리

572 **child** [tʃaild] 어린이

That child is my student. 저 아이는 나의 학생이다.
▶someone who is not yet an adult

More 복수형 children

573 **keep** [kiːp] 유지하다

She kept her promise. 그녀는 그녀의 약속을 지켰다.
▶to continue having or holding something; to continue in a specified state

More 동사변화 keep - kept - kept, keep one's promise 약속을 지키다

574 **why** [hwai] 왜

Why does he like summer? 그는 왜 여름을 좋아하니?
▶for what reason

575 **telephone** [téləfòun] 전화기

May I use this telephone? 이 전화기 좀 써도 될까요?
▶a tool that enables you to speak to someone far away

576 **speak** [spiːk] 말하다

My uncle can speak French. 나의 삼촌은 프랑스어를 말 할 수 있다.
▶to make word with the voice; to say something

More 동사변화 speak - spoke - spoken

CHAPTER 1

UNIT 49

Word 577~588

Shadow Speaking 332

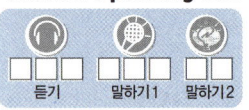

듣기 098 말하기 099

577 bank [bæŋk] 은행

The bank is between the hospital and the bookstore.
그 은행은 그 병원과 그 서점 사이에 있다.
▶ a business where people put their money for safekeeping

578 change [tʃeindʒ] 바꾸다

I want to change my clothes. 나는 나의 옷을 바꾸기를 원한다.
▶ to make something different become different

579 borrow [bɔ́(ː)rou] 빌리다

May I borrow the scissors? 그 가위 좀 빌려 줄래?
▶ to receive something with the intention of later returning it
More lend 빌려주다

580 which [hwitʃ] 어떤, 어떤 것

Which do you like better, an apple or a pear?
너는 사과와 배 중에 어느 것을 더 좋아하니?
▶ what thing in particular

581 date [deit] 날짜

What's the date today? 오늘이 며칠이니?
▶ the month, day, and year of a specified time

582 now [nau] 지금

What time is it now? 지금 몇 시니?
▶ this moment; the present time

UNIT 49

583 **absent** [ǽbsənt] 결석의

He was absent from school. 그는 학교에 결석했다.
▶not being somewhere

584 **who** [hu:] 누구

Who is that boy? 저 소년은 누구니?
▶which or what person

More 의문사 who, when, where, what, how, why

585 **stop** [stɑp] 멈추다, 정지시키다

We stopped the computer game. 우리는 컴퓨터 게임을 멈췄다
▶to put an end to an action, motion, event, etc.

586 **bed** [bed] 침대

My bed is very comfortable. 내 침대는 매우 편하다
▶a piece of furniture that you sleep on

More go to bed 자다

587 **station** [stéiʃən] 역

I will go to the station by subway. 나는 지하철로 역에 갈 것이다.
▶a place where a train, bus, or subway stop so that people or things can get on or off

More police station 경찰서, fire station 소방서, gas station 주유소

588 **understand** [ʌndərstǽnd] 이해하다

I didn't understand the story. 나는 그 이야기를 이해하지 못했다.
▶to know and comprehend something

More 동사변화 understand - understood - understood

Word 960 • 107

CHAPTER 1

UNIT **50** Word **589~600**

듣기 100 말하기 101

589 switch [switʃ] 스위치

Don't forget to turn off the switch. 스위치 끄는 것 잊지 마라.
▶a device used to turn something on or off, usually by pressing it

590 angry [ǽŋgri] 화가 난

He is angry with me. 그는 나에게 화가 나 있다.
▶feeling anger; filled with anger

More 비교변화 angry - angrier - angriest

591 worry [wə́ːri] 걱정, 걱정하다

Don't worry about it. 그것에 대해서 걱정하지 마라.
▶a problem or concern; to think about something a lot

592 computer [kəmpjúːtər] 컴퓨터

I bought a new computer. 나는 새 컴퓨터를 샀다.
▶a device that processes information at a high speed

593 because [bikɔ́ːz] 왜냐하면, ~ 때문에

You can't go there because you are too young.
너는 너무 어리기 때문에 거기에 갈 수 없다.
▶for the reason that

594 tomato [təméitou] 토마토

Tomatoes are good for our health. 토마토는 우리의 건강에 좋다.
▶a red fruit that is used to make ketchup

UNIT 50

595 **greedy** [gríːdi] 욕심 많은

He is a greedy man. 그는 욕심 많은 사람이다.
▶ wanting something more than necessary; having an excessive desire for something

More 비교변화 greedy - greedier - greediest

596 **mountain** [máuntən] 산

I often climb up the mountain. 나는 가끔 등산을 한다.
▶ a part of land that is much higher than its surrounding land

597 **earth** [əːrθ] 지구

Columbus believed that the earth is round.
콜럼버스는 지구는 둥글다고 믿었다.
▶ the third closest planet to the sun

More Mercury 수성, Venus 금성, Mars 화성, Jupiter 목성, Saturn 토성

598 **busy** [bízi] 바쁜

I had a busy day. 나는 바쁜 하루를 보냈다.
▶ being in action; having lots to do

More 비교변화 busy - busier - busiest

599 **winter** [wíntər] 겨울

We went to Japan last winter. 우리는 지난 겨울에 일본에 갔었다.
▶ the season between fall and spring; the coldest season

600 **best** [best] 최고의, 제일 좋은

I always do my best. 나는 언제나 최선을 다한다.
▶ to the fullest of one's ability

Spelling Bee 180

⭐ **[1-30]** 단어의 의미를 읽고, 알맞은 단어를 쓰세요. (Unit 01-08)

1. _____ : having a lower temperature than what is considered cool

2. _____ : scared of something

3. _____ : to put word on paper with a writing tool

4. _____ : to stay in one place until one arrives

5. _____ : the standard unit of money used in the US, Canada, australia, and other countries

6. _____ : someone who you know and like very much and enjoy spending time with

7. _____ : to hold and move something towards you

8. _____ : a table that is use to read, write and work

9. _____ : being apart from something

10. _____ : at a time following; at a time later than

11. _____ : a rectangle with all four sides having the same length

12. _____ : having little or no strength

13. _____ : a person who cooks; to prepare food by heating it

14. _____ : to change into; to come to be

15. _____ : to give a name to something; to reach someone by telephone

16. _____ : to place something somewhere

17. _____ : the warmest season of the year the season between spring and fall

18. _____ : to move at a fast speed using the legs and feet; faster than a walk

19. _____ : having no empty space; satisfied with food or drink

20. _____ : one of the two parts of your face you use to see

21. _____ : to exchange something for money

22. _____ : feeling of wanting food

23. _____ : prepared to do something

24. _____ : a large farm animal that is raised for its milk and meat

25. _____ : small sticks that are used in pairs to grasp food

26. _____ : to give money for something you buy or for a service

27. _____ : the space around the earth where you can see the clouds

28. _____ : feeling the need to drink something

29. _____ : a period of seven days

30. _____ : to become someone's husband or wife

Spelling Bee 180

[31-60] 단어의 의미를 읽고, 알맞은 단어를 쓰세요. (Unit 09-16)

31. _____ : the direction that is right of the sunrise

32. _____ : a place that sells things store

33. _____ : by way of; by means of

34. _____ : good things that happen to you by chance, not because of your own efforts or abilities

35. _____ : having a high temperature; the opposite of cold

36. _____ : to get someone to stop sleeping; to stop sleeping

37. _____ : big in size

38. _____ : a drawing, painting, or photo of someone or something

39. _____ : to stop living

40. _____ : to show your appreciation to someone

41. _____ : used to express regret

42. _____ : at a high speed; going at a high speed

43. _____ : allowed to do or be anything; costing no money

44. _____ : a food that is made from a mixture of flour and water and usually baked

45. _____ : to give a solution to a question or problem

46. _____ : a place where animals are kept for people to see

47. _____ : paper or coins used for buying and selling

48. _____ : the female ruler of a country led by a royal family or the wife of a king

49. _____ : to say the numbers in order; to find the number of things involved

50. _____ : having an acid taste or smell like a lemon, etc.

51. _____ : not feeling well

52. _____ : information about what just happened

53. _____ : intelligent; well-educated

54. _____ : to understand something fully

55. _____ : very unpleasant to look at; the opposite of pretty

56. _____ : having little energy; feeling a need to rest

57. _____ : everything; the whole

58. _____ : a place, often outside, where many kinds of things are sold by people

59. _____ : a writing tool made of a soft rock that is used on boards

60. _____ : to discover; to come upon after looking for

Spelling Bee 180

⭐ **[61-90]** 단어의 의미를 읽고, 알맞은 단어를 쓰세요. (Unit 17-24)

61. _____ : to show joy or amusement with a smile and a chuckle or explosive sound

62. _____ : someone who studies, especially at a school

63. _____ : an instrument with black and white keys and three pedals that you can press to create music

64. _____ : the direction in which the sun sets; the opposite of east

65. _____ : an animal covered with feathers that has wings and a beak

66. _____ : to press against something in order to move it

67. _____ : a plant that has petals and leaves

68. _____ : large in size; the opposite of small

69. _____ : an amount of time that lasts 60 seconds

70. _____ : the color of leaves, grass, etc.

71. _____ : a seat with four legs and a back for one person

72. _____ : to use strength or ability to get something done

73. _____ : to move in the air without touching the ground

74. _____ : an adult female lady; the opposite of man

75. _____ : the part the body between the neck and the stomach area

76. _____ : the things that people wear to cover their body or keep warm

77. _____ : an instrument other than a watch that shows the time

78. _____ : to have on one's body, as in clothing or jewelry

79. _____ : a person who cares for people's teeth, jaws and mouths

80. _____ : to help someone learn something

81. _____ : an object that produces light by using electricity, oil, or gas weighing little

82. _____ : showing grief and unhappiness

83. _____ : a container that is made for holding and drinking liquid

84. _____ : a seed or pod of a plant from the legume family

85. _____ : a long animal that has a narrow body, scaly skin, and no arms or legs

86. _____ : a piece of land that is used for growing plants or letting animals feed on grass

87. _____ : a thick paste that is made by cooking fruit with sugar

88. _____ : something that you wear on your feet for walking

89. _____ : to take something or somebody with oneself

90. _____ : the side or direction that is west of you when you face north

Spelling Bee 180

⭐ **[91-120]** 단어의 의미를 읽고, 알맞은 단어를 쓰세요. (Unit 25-32)

91. _____ : something made to sit on

92. _____ : an object on which food is served

93. _____ : to make clean using water and soap

94. _____ : something that floats and can carry a person over water

95. _____ : to care for deeply and be devoted to

96. _____ : a shell containing an unborn animal which is laid by birds

97. _____ : pure; having no dirt; to remove the dirt from something

98. _____ : a round deep dish

99. _____ : a kind of object or liquid used for cleaning

100. _____ : near the beginning of a period of time; before the expected time

101. _____ : the time of day following the afternoon and before midnight

102. _____ : the area outside of cities and towns; a nation

103. _____ : being small in width; slender

104. _____ : a group of connected carriages that move on a railroad

105. _____ : a food that is made of two slices of bread with food between the slices

106. _____ : a person whose job it is to care for people's health

107. _____ : a building that one or a few families live in

108. _____ : the mother of one's mother or father

109. _____ : the flesh of a dead animal that can be eaten

110. _____ : one of the five thin parts of your hand

111. _____ : a clear liquid that has very little taste and is necessary for things to live

112. _____ : a room or building where things are sold

113. _____ : a vehicle with two wings that can fly in the air

114. _____ : having too much weight

115. _____ : polite word for a female adult woman

116. _____ : an activity that you regularly do for pleasure

117. _____ : coverings that are worn over the feet

118. _____ : going at a high speed

119. _____ : having a lot of money; the opposite of poor

120. _____ : costing a lot of money; the opposite of cheap

Spelling Bee 180

⭐ **[121-150]** 단어의 의미를 읽고, 알맞은 단어를 쓰세요. (Unit 33-40)

121. _____ : the part of the body between the head and shoulders

122. _____ : a motion picture

123. _____ : not feeling well; ill

124. _____ : having no moisture; the opposite of wet

125. _____ : a shoe that covers the foot and part of the leg

126. _____ : a piece of furniture consisting of a flat board on legs

127. _____ : to move along with music

128. _____ : the earth and everything on it

129. _____ : rhythmic sounds made by singing or playing an instrument

130. _____ : an instrument that is shaken to make a ringing sound

131. _____ : the direction that is left of the sunrise

132. _____ : to have one's body develop over time

133. _____ : having a large length or duration

134. _____ : a smooth or polished surface that reflects images

135. _____ : a body of salt water that is smaller than an ocean

136. _____ : a gray or white body floating in the sky that create rain

137. _____ : a group of people that includes parents and their children

138. _____ : a written message that is sent to someone; a symbol that represents a sound from a language

139. _____ : to go to see someone or some place

140. _____ : a length of time that is 365 days

141. _____ : to come or go after someone or something

142. _____ : the part of the face that is used for smelling or breathing

143. _____ : to divide something with a knife, scissors etc.

144. _____ : to gain knowledge of something through study, instruction or experience

145. _____ : to rest on one's bottom such as in a chair or on a sofa

146. _____ : to use your hands to grasp and hold

147. _____ : to pay attention to sound

148. _____ : to hand something to someone; to move past someone or something

149. _____ : a place where lines meet

150. _____ : a set of steps between two or more floors

Spelling Bee 180

⭐ **[151-180]** 단어의 의미를 읽고, 알맞은 단어를 쓰세요. (Unit 41-50)

151. _____ : a road in a city or town where cars are able to travel

152. _____ : to give money to get something

153. _____ : a room used for cooking

154. _____ : a place where people grow flowers or plants

155. _____ : heated at a comfortable level

156. _____ : the part of the day when there is no light

157. _____ : looking beautiful in a sweet way

158. _____ : 12 o'clock in the middle of the day

159. _____ : a piece of music or the Word set to that piece

160. _____ : to do something with an object to get something done

161. _____ : something that is difficult to deal with

162. _____ : a game that is played with rackets and a ligh ball by two or more players on a court with a low net in the middle

163. _____ : being ten more than ninety

164. _____ : a plant that can be eaten that is not a fruit or seed

165. _____ : to start doing something

166. _____ : a sweet food made of mainly sugar

167. _____ : to sit or stand on top of an object while it is moving

168. _____ : to desire to have or do something

169. _____ : a place where doctors and nurses help sick people

170. _____ : something which is eaten and is necessary for life

171. _____ : the season between summer and winter; to drop down a high place

172. _____ : a human; a human being

173. _____ : any particular area of ground; to return to the ground (airplanes, ships)

174. _____ : a tool that enables you to speak to someone far away

175. _____ : to make something different become different

176. _____ : not being somewhere

177. _____ : to know and comprehend something

178. _____ : feeling anger; filled with anger

179. _____ : a problem or concern; to think about something a lot

180. _____ : to the fullest of one's ability

Chapter 2

초등 영단어 960은 영어 단어장이 아닙니다.
Shadow Speaking 332학습을 기반으로 영단어를 통해 영어를 익히도록 설계된 신개념 학습법입니다.

[빈도수 높은 영단어] 360
Unit 51~80

Listening

Speaking 1

Speaking 2

영단어와 문장, 영영풀이를 동시에 학습
Word 601~960

학습한 내용은 **Weekly Test**와 **Spelling Bee**를 통해 자신의 실력을 확인하며 익혀 보세요.

Shadw Speaking 332학습
① 오디어 3번 듣기
② 책을 보며 3번 따라 말하기
③ 책을 보지 않고 2번 따라 말하기

CHAPTER 2

UNIT 51 Word 601~612

---

601 hairpin [hɛ́ərpìn] 머리핀

I have a pretty hairpin. 나는 예쁜 머리핀을 가지고 있다.
▶something that you can close around your hair to keep it in place

602 ticket [tíkit] 표, 입장권

He bought two theater tickets. 그는 극장표 2장을 샀다.
▶a piece of paper that enables you to get into the theatre and watch the movie

603 hurt [həːrt] 다치게 하다

I hurt my hands yesterday. 나는 어제 내 손을 다쳤다.
▶to cause damage to

More 동사변화 hurt - hurt - hurt

604 peace [piːs] 평화

They are longing for peace. 그들은 평화를 갈망하고 있다.
▶a state in which there is no war or fighting

605 yard [jɑːrd] 마당

The children are playing in the yard.
그 어린이들이 마당에서 놀고 있다.
▶an area of land that is next to a building

606 tulip [tjúːlip] 튤립

This is a flower called a tulip. 이것은 튤립이라고 하는 꽃이다.
▶a brightly colored flower that is shaped like a cup

UNIT 51

607 knight [nait] 기사

He was a brave knight. 그는 용감한 기사였다.
▶ a person trained to fight who works for a noble person or a king

608 woods [wudz] 숲

The men went for a walk in the woods.
그 남자들은 숲 속에서 산책을 했다.
▶ a forest; an area with many trees

More wood 나무, 목재

609 war [wɔːr] 전쟁

People don't want war. 사람들은 전쟁을 원하지 않는다.
▶ fight between countries that involves the use of weapons like guns

610 toe [tou] 발가락

Can you touch your toes? 너의 발가락을 만질 수 있나요?
▶ a digit of the foot

More foot 발, hand 손, finger 손가락

611 plant [plænt] 식물, 심다

All plants need light and water. 모든 식물은 빛과 물을 필요로 한다.
▶ something living that cannot move or feel, such as a tree, flower, etc.; to put a seed or plant in the ground to grow

612 blow [blou] 불다

A cold wind blew from the west. 찬 바람이 서쪽에서 불어왔다.
▶ to be blowing; to be moving (air)

More 동사변화 blow - blew - blown

CHAPTER 2

UNIT 52

Word 613~624

Shadow Speaking 332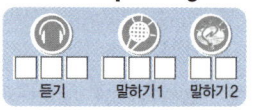

듣기 104 말하기 105

613 photo [fóutou] 사진

She took a photo with him. 그녀는 그와 사진을 찍었다.
▶ a picture taken with a camera; short for photograph

614 gas [gæs] 기체, 가스

Oxygen is gas. 산소는 기체이다.
▶ a liquid that is burned to provide energy for cooking, heating, etc.

615 storm [stɔ:rm] 폭풍우, 폭풍

It looks like a storm is coming. 폭풍우가 올 것 같다.
▶ an occurrence of bad weather in which there is a lot of rain, snow, etc. and often strong winds

616 space [speis] 우주

They want to travel into space. 그들은 우주를 여행하기를 원한다.
▶ an area above the earth where the stars and other planets are

617 drum [drʌm] 드럼

Eric can play the drum. Eric은 드럼을 연주할 수 있다.
▶ an instrument with a skin stretched over the frame

618 example [igzǽmpəl] 예, 보기

Example is better than precept. 실례는 교훈보다 낫다. (속담)
▶ someone or something that is mentioned to help explain what you are saying or to show that a general statement is true

UNIT 52

619 pool [puːl] 수영장

We swam in the pool yesterday. 우리는 어제 수영장에서 수영을 했다.
▶a big container that is bigger than a bathtub and filled with water for swimming

620 piece [piːs] 조각, 일부분

She cut the cake in eight pieces. 그녀는 케이크를 8조각으로 잘랐다.
▶a part that has been divided from the whole More a piece of

More a piece of pizza 피자 한 조각, pieces of glass 유리 조각들

621 steal [stiːl] 훔치다

He stole the book from the bookstore. 그는 서점에서 그 책을 훔쳤다.
▶to take something without permission

More 동사변화 steal - stole - stolen

622 salt [sɔːlt] 소금

Pass me the salt, please. 소금 좀 건네주세요.
▶a white powder that is added to food to make it taste better

623 math [mæθs] 수학

We have math class today. 오늘 수학 수업이 있다.
▶the study of numbers, shapes and logic; short for mathematics

More mathematician 수학자

624 kid [kid] 아이, 청소년

She is a smart kid. 그녀는 영리한 아이이다.
▶an informal way of saying child

CHAPTER 2

UNIT 53 Word 625~636

Shadow Speaking 332

---

625 twins [twins] 쌍둥이

They are twins. 그들은 쌍둥이다.
▶ two people who look exactly the same; two people who share the same DNA

626 test [test] 시험, 검사

I had a math test today. 나는 오늘 수학 시험을 봤다.
▶ a set of questions or problems that are designed to measure a person's knowledge, skills, or abilities

627 baker [béikər] 제빵사, 빵집주인

Mr. Brown is a baker. Brown 씨는 제빵사이다.
▶ a person who makes bread

More bakery 제과점, bake 빵을 굽다

628 bedroom [bédrù:m] 침실, 방

We have three bedrooms. 우리는 침실이 3개 있다.
▶ a room where people sleep; a room with a bed

629 dig [dig] 파다

He and I dug a hole. 그와 나는 구멍을 팠다.
▶ to pick up and remove dirt from the ground

More 동사변화 dig - dug - dug

630 scared [skɛərd] 무서운

The boy is scared of going out alone.
그 소년은 혼자 밖에 나가는 것을 무서워한다.
▶ afraid of something; frightened

UNIT 53

631 lake [leik] 호수

There are many fishes in the lake.
그 호수에는 많은 종류의 물고기들이 있다.
▶a large area of water surrounded by land

632 order [ɔ́:rdər] 명령하다, 명령

The officer ordered the soldiers to fire.
그 장교는 그 군인들에게 발포하라고 명령했다.
▶to give a command; an instruction or direction that must be obeyed

633 pebble [pébəl] 조약돌, 자갈

There are many pebbles in the river. 강에는 많은 조약돌이 있다.
▶a small stone that is larger than sand

634 leave [li:v] 떠나다, 남겨두다

The plane leaves for Seoul at twelve.
그 비행기는 12시에 서울을 향해 떠난다.
▶to go away; to let something stay behind

More 동사변화 leave - left - left, arrive 도착하다

635 kite [kait] 연

I like to fly a kite with my friends.
나는 친구들과 연 날리는 것을 좋아한다.
▶a light flying object tied to a string which a person holds on the ground

636 grass [græs, grɑ:s] 풀, 잔디

Cows feed on grass. 젖소는 풀을 먹는다.
▶a plant that has thin, green leaves that cover the ground

CHAPTER 2

UNIT 54

Word 637~648

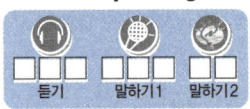

Shadow Speaking 332

듣기 108 말하기 109

637 noise [nɔiz] 소음, 잡음

Don't make a noise. 떠들지 마라.
▶ a loud sound

638 during [djúəriŋ] ··· 동안

I studied hard during my summer vacation.
나는 여름 방학 동안 열심히 공부했다.
▶ while doing something; within a certain time period

639 restaurant [réstərənt] 식당

The restaurant is between the bank and the bookstore.
그 식당은 은행과 서점 사이에 있다.
▶ a business where people can buy and eat food

640 heart [ha:rt] 심장, 가슴

My sister had a weak heart. 나의 여동생은 심장이 약하다.
▶ the part of your body that pumps blood

641 ax [æks] 도끼

He chopped the tree with an ax. 그는 도끼로 나무를 잘랐다.
▶ a stick with a heavy blade, usually used for cutting trees and wood

642 pipe [paip] 관, 파이프

This is a gas pipe. 이것은 가스관이다.
▶ a hard tube that is used to carry water or oil, etc. to another place

UNIT 54

643 · hit [hit] 치다

He hit the nail with the hammer. 그는 망치로 못을 쳤다.
▶to touch upon something with force

More 동사변화 hit - hit - hit

644 · fresh [freʃ] 신선한

I like fresh vegetables. 나는 신선한 야채를 좋아한다.
▶newly made, produced, etc.; not old, spoild, etc

More 비교변화 fresh - fresher - freshest

645 · deer [diər] 사슴

The king hunted the deer. 그 왕은 그 사슴을 사냥했다.
▶a furry animal that is usually brown with four hooved legs and horns on the male

More 복수형 deer

646 · copy [kápi] 복사하다

I copied a document. 나는 서류를 복사했다.
▶to make a likeness of

647 · top [tɑp] 맨 위, 꼭대기

The book is on top of the shelf. 그 책은 선반 맨 위에 있다.
▶the highest part of something

More on top of ~의 위에

648 · hole [houl] 구덩이, 구멍

He dug a deep hole in the ground. 그는 땅에 깊은 구멍을 팠다.
▶an opening in something

CHAPTER 2

UNIT 55 — Word 649~660

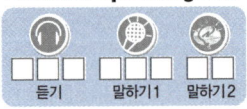

듣기 110 말하기 111

649 If [if] 만약 ~라면

If it rains, I will not go on a picnic.
만약 비가 오면, 난 소풍을 가지 않을 것이다.
▶ in the event that; on condition that; whether

650 little [lítl] 작은, 소규모의

My uncle has a little farm. 나의 삼촌은 작은 농장이 있다.
▶ small; tiny; the opposite of big

More 비교변화 little - less - least

651 toward [tɔːrd] ~ 쪽으로, ~을 향하여

They went toward the river. 그들은 강 쪽으로 갔다.
▶ in the direction of

652 lie [lai] 거짓말, 거짓말을 하다

Don't lie to me. 나한테 거짓말을 하지 마라.
▶ something that is not true; to tell a lie

More 동사변화 lie - lied - lied

653 musician [mjuːzíʃən] 음악가

He is a jazz musician. 그는 재즈 음악가이다.
▶ a person who makes music

654 hide [haid] 숨기다, 감추다

She hid the letter in a bag. 그녀는 그 편지를 가방에 감췄다.
▶ to move to or be in a place that other people cannot see

More 동사변화 hide - hid - hidden

UNIT 55

655 strange [streindʒ] 이상한, 낯선

I met a strange man on my way home.
나는 집에 오는 길에 이상한 남자를 만났다.
▶being different from what you usually see

More 비교변화 strange - stranger - strangest

656 appear [əpíər] 나타나다

She appeared at five o'clock. 그녀는 5시에 모습을 나타냈다.
▶to come into sight; to become visible

More appearance 모습, 외모

657 sunny [sʌ́ni] 화창한, 맑은

It will be sunny tomorrow. 내일은 맑을 것이다.
▶full of sunshine

658 drive [draiv] 운전하다

My mom can drive the car well. 나의 엄마는 차를 잘 운전하신다.
▶to control a car or other vehicle

More 동사변화 drive - drove - driven

659 empty [émpti] 비어 있는, 빈

There are many empty houses in the city.
그 도시에는 빈 집들이 많이 있다.
▶without anything inside

More 비교변화 empty - emptier - emptiest

660 supermarket [súːpərmàːrkit] 슈퍼마켓

I bought fruit at a supermarket. 나는 슈퍼마켓에서 과일을 샀다.
▶a store that sells food and other things that you need for your home

Word 960

CHAPTER 2

UNIT 56 Word 661~672

Shadow Speaking 332

661 coin [kɔin] 동전
My hobby is collecting coins. 나의 취미는 동전 모으는 것이다.
▶money made from metal, usually in the shape of a circle

662 ghost [goust] 유령
She is afraid of ghosts. 그녀는 유령을 두려워한다.
▶the soul of a dead person which is visible to living people

663 apartment [əpá:rtmənt] 아파트
They moved into the new apartment.
그들은 새 아파트로 이사했다.
▶a room or group of rooms in a building that houses people

664 famous [féiməs] 유명한
He is a famous artist. 그는 유명한 화가이다.
▶well known by many people
More 비교변화 famous - more famous - most famous

665 choose [tʃu:z] 택하다, 고르다
We chose him for our leader. 우리는 그를 우리의 지도자로 뽑았다.
▶to select; to decide upon a thing or things among several
More 동사변화 choose - chose - chosen

666 fake [feik] 가짜의, 거짓된
This is fake money. 이것은 위조지폐이다.
▶not real; not genuine

UNIT 56

667 present [prézənt] 선물, 현재

She bought a birthday present for her mother.
그녀는 그녀의 어머니를 위해 생일 선물을 샀다.
▶something that you give to someone: the current time

668 invite [inváit] 초대하다

They invited me to the wedding. 그들은 나를 결혼식에 초대했다.
▶to request someone to join you in doing something or to come to your home

More invitation 초대, invitation card 초대장

669 dangerous [déindʒərəs] 위험한

It is dangerous to swim in this river.
이 강에서 수영하는 것은 위험하다.
▶involving danger or risk; not safe

More 비교변화 dangerous - more dangerous - most dangerous, danger 위험

670 bench [bentʃ] 벤치, 긴 의자

There are many benches in the park. 그 공원에는 벤치가 많다.
▶a long, hard seat that can hold a few people

671 line [lain] 선, 줄, 라인

Draw a thick black line on the page.
그 페이지 위에 굵게 검은색 선을 그어라.
▶a string-like shape

672 rocket [rákit] 로켓

They are carrying the rocket. 그들은 로켓을 운반하고 있다.
▶a vehicle that is shaped like a cylinder that goes up in the air after it is lit with fire

CHAPTER 2

UNIT 57

Word 673~684

Shadow Speaking 332

듣기 114 말하기 115

673 **explain** [ikspléin] 설명하다

He **explained** the rules of the game first.
그는 먼저 그 경기의 규칙들을 설명했다.
▶ to make clear or easy to understand

674 **careful** [kɛ́ərfəl] 주의 깊은

She is very **careful** with her work. 그녀는 하는 일에 매우 주의 깊다.
▶ using care; with care

More 비교변화 careful - more careful - most careful

675 **goddess** [gádis] 여신

Minerva is the **goddess** of wisdom. 미네르바는 지혜의 여신이다.
▶ a female god

676 **patient** [péiʃənt] 환자, 병자

The **patient** will get well soon. 그 환자는 금방 나을 것이다.
▶ someone who needs medical care

677 **greet** [gri:t] 인사하다, 환영하다

They **greeted** me with a smile. 그들은 나를 미소로 환영했다.
▶ to say hello to someone

678 **wish** [wiʃ] 소망, 바라다, 희망하다

I **wish** to go abroad. 나는 외국에 가고 싶다.
▶ a hope for something; to want something to be true

UNIT 57

679 **exercise** [éksərsàiz] 운동하다, 운동

How often do you exercise? 당신은 얼마나 자주 운동을 하나요?
▶ to move one's body for health; physical activity that is done to become stronger and healthier

680 **foolish** [fú:liʃ] 어리석은

She is just a foolish woman. 그녀는 그저 어리석은 여자이다.
▶ stupid; not wise

More 비교변화 foolish - more foolish - most foolish

681 **club** [klʌb] 클럽, 동호회

I want to join a tennis club. 나는 테니스 클럽에 가입하기를 원한다.
▶ a group of people that meet for a common purpose

682 **guest** [gest] 손님

Ashley was not on the guest list.
Ashley는 손님 명단에 들어 있지 않았다.
▶ a person who is a visitor somewhere

683 **forgive** [fərgív] 용서하다

He forgave the boy for stealing the toy car.
그는 그 소년이 그 장난감 차를 훔친 것을 용서했다.
▶ to excuse a past wrong

More 동사변화 forgive - forgave - forgiven

684 **fact** [fækt] 사실

The stories are based on real facts.
그 이야기들은 실제 사실들을 근거로 하고 있다.
▶ something that is true

CHAPTER 2

Word 685~696

---

685 dead [ded] 죽은

He has been dead for three years. 그가 죽은 지 3년이 된다.
▶ not living; not alive

686 happen [hǽpən] 발생하다

Accidents will happen. 사고는 일어나기 마련이다.
▶ to take place; to become of

687 without [wiðàut] … 없이

Animals cannot live without air and water.
동물들은 공기와 물 없이 살 수 없다.
▶ used to express absence or lack of

688 quarrel [kwɔ́:rəl] 싸우다, 다투다

He quarreled with his sister for the bag.
그는 누나와 가방을 차지하려고 다투었다.
▶ to have an angry disagreement about something

689 footprint [fútprìnt] 발자국

There were many footprints in the snow.
눈 위에 많은 발자국들이 있었다.
▶ the mark left by one's foot when walking

690 kingdom [kíŋdəm] 왕국

It is the story of an ancient kingdom.
이것은 고대 왕국에 관한 이야기이다.
▶ the land ruled by a king

UNIT 58

691 **handsome** [hǽnsəm] 잘생긴

He is the most handsome man in the class.
그는 반에서 가장 잘생긴 남자이다.
▶good-looking; pleasing to look at

More 비교변화 handsome - handsomer - handsomest

692 **wall** [wɔːl] 벽

I am going to paint the wall white.
나는 벽을 흰색으로 칠할 것이다.
▶a side of a room that starts from the top of the floor to the bottom of the ceiling

693 **fire** [faiər] 불

The animals are afraid of fire. 그 동물들은 불을 두려워한다.
▶the flame that come from something burning

694 **speed** [spiːd] 속도, 속력

He reduced the speed and turned right.
그는 속도를 줄이고 우회전을 했다.
▶the rate of which someone or somthing moves or travels

695 **real** [ríːəl] 진짜의, 실제의

They have a real chance of sucess.
그들은 실제로 성공할 가능성이 있다.
▶true; not imagined; the opposite of fake

696 **soldier** [sóuldʒər] 군인, 병사

Many soldiers helped poor people in the town.
많은 군인들이 그 마을에 있는 가난한 사람들을 도왔다.
▶a person whose job is to protect a country, often by fighting

CHAPTER 2

UNIT 59 — Word 697~708

듣기 118 말하기 119

---

697 fence [fens] 울타리

The man is building a fence. 그 남자는 울타리를 치고 있다.
▶ a wall usually made of wood or wire to stop people or things from entering

---

698 crayon [kréiən] 크레용

The children drew pictures with crayons.
그 어린이들은 크레용으로 그림을 그렸다.
▶ a small stick made of wax, chalk, or charcoal that is used for drawing

---

699 ground [graund] 땅, 지면

The men dug the ground. 그 남자들이 땅을 팠다.
▶ the solid surface of the earth

---

700 stone [stoun] 돌

Many houses are built of stone. 많은 집들이 돌로 지어져 있다.
▶ a small rock

---

701 pineapple [páinæpl] 파인애플

I like pineapple juice. 나는 파인애플 주스를 좋아한다.
▶ a fruit with green, pointy leaves on top and spiky, brown skin with sweet, juicy yellow flesh underneath

---

702 butter [bʌ́tər] 버터

Put the butter in the pan first. 먼저 그 팬에 버터를 넣어라.
▶ a solid yellowish food that is made from the cream of milk

UNIT 59

703 **shape** [ʃeip] 모양

The pool is in the shape of a heart. 그 수영장은 하트 모양이다.
▶ the form or outline of an object

704 **feed** [fiːd] 먹이를 주다

The farmers feed their horses on grass.
그 농부들이 그들의 말에게 풀을 먹인다.
▶ to give food to someone or something

705 **mind** [maind] 마음, 의견, 생각

I have no mind to go for a walk. 나는 산책하고 싶은 생각이 없다.
▶ opinion; thought; the thing which allows us to think

706 **clever** [klévər] 영리한

She is the cleverest girl in the class.
그녀는 방에서 가장 영리한 소녀이다.
▶ showing intelligence or skill

More 비교변화 clever - cleverer - cleverest

707 **stomach** [stʌ́mək] 배, 복부

Don't exercise on a full stomach. 배가 부를 때 운동지하지 마라.
▶ the part of the body that digests food; also the area around the stomach

More stomachache 복통

708 **equal** [íːkwəl] 동일한, 같은

There is an equal member of boys and girls in the class.
그 반에는 남자와 여자가 동일한 숫자이다.
▶ the same in number, amount, degree or quality, etc.

CHAPTER 2

UNIT 60 — Word 709~720

Shadow Speaking 332

듣기 120 말하기 121

709 **feather** [féðər] 깃털

The little girl was as light as a feather.
그 작은 소녀는 깃털처럼 가벼웠다.
▶ the thing which covers birds and no other animal

710 **board** [bɔːrd] 판자, 널

I played with my friends on the big board.
나는 친구들과 큰 판자 위에서 놀았다.
▶ a long, flat piece of a hard material

711 **select** [silékt] 선택하다

She selected the present for her son.
그녀는 아들의 생일 선물을 골랐다.
▶ to decide upon a thing or things among several

712 **silver** [sílvər] 은, 은색의

Jonathan won a silver medal. Jonathan은 은메달을 차지했다.
▶ a valuable gray-colored metal; the color of this metal

713 **mailman** [méilmən] 우체부, 우편배달원

The mailman comes round once a day.
그 우편배달원은 하루에 한 번 온다.
▶ a man who delivers mail

714 **prince** [prins] 왕자

The prince is brave and clever. 그 왕자는 용감하고 똑똑하다.
▶ the son of a king and queen

UNIT 60

715 cheese [tʃiːz] 치즈

Look at the camera and say "cheese."
카메라를 보고 "치즈"라고 말하세요.
▶a solid or creamy food made from the solid part of milk

716 university [jùːnəvə́ːrsəti] 대학

His daughter entered the university. 그의 딸은 대학에 들어갔다.
▶an institution of education people can attend after high school

717 sheep [ʃiːp] 양

Sheep were running in the fields. 양들이 들판에서 뛰고 있었다.
▶an animal with thick, curly fur that is raised on a farm for its meat and wool

More 복수형 sheep, lamb 어린 양

718 art [ɑːrt] 미술, 예술

Judy is good at art and design. Judy는 미술과 디자인을 잘한다.
▶an expression of creativity; things which are created to be beautiful

719 rose [rouz] 장미

The rose is the prettiest flower in my garden.
장미는 내 정원에서 가장 아름다운 꽃이다.
▶a flower with a sweet smell that is usually white, yellow, red, or pink and which has thorns on the stem

720 grape [greip] 포도

We like grapes and kiwis. 우리는 포도와 키위를 좋아한다.
▶a fruit that grows on a vine, which is usually purple in Korea and can be used to make jam, juice, jelly, wine and oil

CHAPTER 2

UNIT 61 — Word 721~732

Shadow Speaking 332

듣기 122 말하기 123

721 wise [waiz] 현명한

There live a wise old man in the town.
그 마을에 현명한 노인이 살았다.
▶full of wisdom

More 비교변화 wise - wiser - wisest, wisdom 지혜

722 enter [éntər] 들어가다

Someone entered the room. 누군가 방으로 들어갔다.
▶to go or come into something

723 ink [iŋk] 잉크

The boy wrote with a pen and ink. 그 소년은 펜과 잉크로 썼다.
▶the liquid put in pens so that you can write with them

724 total [tóutl] 총액, 합계

The total number of the apples was ten.
그 사과의 총 개수는 10개였다.
▶the number or amount of everything counted

725 beach [bi:tʃ] 해변, 바닷가

They are playing soccer on the beach.
그들은 바닷가에서 축구를 하고 있다.
▶the sandy land along a sea or ocean

726 only [óunli] 오직, 단지

you can only guess. 너는 오직 추측할 수밖에 없다.
▶no other; no more than

UNIT 61

727 **hen** [hen] 암탉

<u>Hens</u> lay eggs. 암탉이 알을 낳는다.
▶a female chicken

More cock, rooster 수탉, chick 병아리

728 **note** [nout] 메모, 쪽지

She made a <u>note</u> on a piece of paper.
그녀는 한 장의 종이에 메모를 했다.
▶a little message that is written

729 **calendar** [kǽlindər] 달력

He marked the date on a <u>calendar</u>. 그는 달력에 그 날짜를 표시했다.
▶something that tells you the months of a year as well as the days of each month and the order they come in

730 **coat** [kout] 코트

Put on your <u>coat</u>. 너의 코트를 입어라.
▶a long piece of clothing that covers the bottom of your neck to the waist or below that is usually worn over other clothes to keep warm

731 **repeat** [ripíːt] 반복하다

Can you <u>repeat</u> your question?
당신의 질문을 다시 말씀해 주시겠습니까?
▶to do again

732 **bus** [bʌs] 버스

I go to school by <u>bus</u>. 나는 버스로 학교에 간다.
▶a big, long car that can carry at least several people to take them to the planned location

CHAPTER 2

UNIT 62 — Word 733~744

Shadow Speaking 332

733 **birthday** [bə́ːrθdèi] 생일

When is your birthday? 너의 생일은 언제이니?
▶ the month and day that one was born

734 **leaf** [liːf] 나뭇잎

The ground was covered with dead leaves.
땅은 낙엽으로 덮여 있었다.
▶ the part of a plant that absorbs sunlight; the part of a plant or tree that falls off in autumn

More 복수형 leaves

735 **decide** [disáid] 결정하다

He decided where to go. 그는 어디로 갈지 결정했다.
▶ to make a choice about

More decision 결정

736 **place** [pleis] 장소, 곳

This is a good place for a picnic. 여기는 소풍으로 좋은 장소이다.
▶ a certain space; an area; a location

737 **human** [hjúːmən] 인간, 사람

Dogs can run faster than humans. 개는 사람보다 빨리 달릴 수 있다.
▶ a person

738 **fool** [fuːl] 바보

Don't be such a fool. 그렇게 바보같이 굴지 마라.
▶ a stupid person

UNIT 62

739 step [step] 걸음, 단계

She took a step toward the window.
그녀는 창문을 향해 걸음을 걸었다.
▶ the act of moving forward and putting down one's foot once; the distance of this action

740 beside [bisáid] … 옆에

My house is beside the post office. 나의 집은 우체국 옆에 있다.
▶ next to; by the side of

More besides … 외에(는)

741 interesting [íntəristiŋ] 재미있는, 흥미 있는

This story is very interesting. 이 이야기는 매우 재미있다.
▶ holding one's attention

More 비교변화 interesting - more interesting - most interesting, interest 관심, 흥미

742 scorpion [skɔ́ːrpiən] 전갈

Scorpions have a long tail. 전갈은 긴 꼬리를 가지고 있다.
▶ a small animal with eight legs and a tail that contains poison

743 princess [prinsés] 공주

The knight danced with a princess. 그 기사는 공주와 춤을 추었다.
▶ the daughter of a king and queen

744 plan [plæn] 계획하다, 계획

We plan to go to Jeju-do during summer vacation.
우리는 여름방학 동안에 제주도에 갈 계획이다.
▶ to have an intention to do something; to make details for a course of action; somthing that a person intends to do

CHAPTER 2

UNIT 63 — Word 745~756

Shadow Speaking 332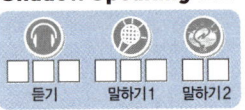

듣기 126 말하기 127

745 giant [dʒáiənt] 거인

Jack is running away from the giant.
Jack은 그 거인으로부터 도망치고 있다.
▶ a very large person

746 bone [boun] 뼈, 뼈다귀

This fish has a lot of bones in it. 이 생선은 뼈가 많다.
▶ the hard, white parts of the body that make up the skeleton

747 also [ɔ́ːlsou] 또한, 역시

I also like to ride a bike. 나 또한 자전거 타는 것을 좋아한다.
▶ in addition; additionally; too

748 object [ábdʒikt] 물건, 물체

My brother pointed to a distant object.
나의 남동생은 멀리 있는 물건을 가리켰다.
▶ a thing; an item

749 wife [waif] 아내, 부인

He sometimes goes to the market with his wife.
그는 때때로 아내와 함께 시장에 간다.
▶ the woman a man is married to; a married woman

750 dream [driːm] 꿈, 꿈꾸다

My dreams will come true. 나의 꿈은 이루어질 것이다.
▶ a vision that you have when you sleep; to have as a desire or ambition

UNIT 63

751 **near** [niər] 가까운

My school is very near. 나의 학교는 아주 가깝다.
▶close to someone or something in distance

More 비교변화 near - nearer - nearest

752 **fight** [fait] 싸움, 싸우다

Let's have a snowball fight now. 지금 눈싸움을 하자.
▶a violent physical struggle between opponents; to use weapon or physical force to try to hurt someone

753 **punish** [pʌ́niʃ] 벌주다, 처벌하다

They are here to punish him. 그들은 그를 벌주기 위해 여기에 왔다.
▶to give a penalty to

More punishment (처벌)

754 **lamb** [læm] 어린 양

He stole the lamb yesterday. 그는 어제 어린 양을 훔쳤다.
▶a young sheep

755 **pyramid** [pírəmìd] 피라미드

I looked at the biggest pyramid in Egypt.
나는 이집트에서 가장 큰 피라미드를 보았다.
▶a shape with a polygon for a base and triangular sides that meet together at the top

756 **ladder** [lǽdər] 사다리

He is climbing up the ladder. 그는 그 사다리를 올라가고 있다.
▶a setting of steps between two sticks or poles and which go straight up

CHAPTER 2

UNIT 64 — Word 757~768

Shadow Speaking 332

---

757 **sound** [saund] 소리, 음

She heard the sound of footsteps. 그녀는 발자국 소리를 들었다.
▶something that the ears can hear

758 **forget** [fərgét] 잊다

I never forget a face. 나는 사람들의 얼굴을 절대 안 잊어버린다.
▶to be unable to think of or remember

More 동사변화 forget - forgot - forgotten

759 **few** [fju:] (수가) 많지 않은, 적은

There were few passengers in the bus. 버스에는 승객이 거의 없다.
▶small in number

More (양이) 많지 않은 little

760 **palace** [pǽlis] 궁전

The palace is beautiful and wonderful.
그 궁전은 아름답고 굉장했다.
▶a kind of large house or mansion used by a leader of a nation

761 **ice** [ais] 얼음

There was ice on the door. 그 문에 얼음이 있었다.
▶frozen water

762 **card** [kɑːrd] 두꺼운 종이, 카드

She gave me a birthday card. 그녀가 나에게 생일 카드를 줬다.
▶a small, stiff piece of paper

UNIT 64

763 brave [breiv] 용감한

The prince is very brave. 그 왕자는 매우 용감하다.
▶having a lot of courage; willing to take risks or face danger

More 비교변화 brave - braver - bravest, bravery 용감, 용기

764 gather [gǽðər] 모으다, 모이다

Many people gathered in the square. 많은 사람들이 광장에 모였다.
▶to bring together into a group

765 build [bild] 짓다, 건설하다

He built a house for his parents. 그는 그의 부모님을 위해 집을 지었다.
▶to make something by putting things together

More 동사변화 build - built - built

766 jungle [dʒʌ́ŋgl] 정글, 밀림

The lion is the king of the jungle. 사자는 밀림의 왕이다.
▶a tropical rain forest that has a lot of plants growing closely together

767 bridge [bridʒ] 다리

We crossed the bridge over the river.
우리는 강 위에 있는 다리를 건넜다.
▶something flat that lies above land or water that people are able to walk on to get from one side to the other

768 captain [kǽptin] 선장, 주장

He was the captain of our team. 그는 우리 팀의 주장이었다.
▶a person who is in charge of a ship or an airplane; an athlete who is chosen to be the leader of a team

Word 960 · 151

CHAPTER 2

UNIT 65 Word 769~780

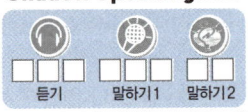

듣기 130 말하기 131

769 **hall** [hɔːl] 홀, 복도

There are three halls in the museum. 박물관에는 3개의 홀이 있다.
▶ a room that is built to connect other rooms to each other

770 **travel** [trǽvəl] 여행하다

He traveled around the world last year.
그는 작년에 세계일주 여행을 했다.
▶ to go from one place to another

771 **fold** [fould] 접다

She folded the paper in half. 그녀는 그 종이를 반으로 접었다.
▶ to lay one part over another

More unfold 펴다

772 **classmate** [klǽsmèit] 급우, 반 친구

Alice is my classmate. Alice는 나의 반 친구이다.
▶ a student in the same class as another

773 **gentle** [dʒéntl] 온화한, 순한

His father is gentle with children. 그의 아버지는 아이들에게 다정하다.
▶ soft in manner

More 비교변화 gentle - gentler - gentlest

774 **print** [print] 인쇄하다, 프린트를 하다

I'm printing the document. 나는 그 문서를 인쇄하고 있다.
▶ to use a printer to recreate word or pictures on paper

UNIT 65

775 bath [bæθ] 목욕, 욕조

He likes to have a bath. 그는 목욕하는 것을 좋아한다.
▶ the act or process of washing yourself in a bathtub filled with water

776 island [áilənd] 섬

The airplane landed on a small island.
그 비행기는 작은 섬에 착륙했다.
▶ a small area of land surrounded by water

777 tower [táuər] 탑, 타워

When I was in Paris, I wanted to go to the Eiffel Tower.
나는 파리에 갔을 때 에펠탑에 가고 싶었다.
▶ a building that is higher than its diameter

778 next [nekst] 다음의

We will go to the zoo next Saturday.
우리는 다음 주 토요일에 동물원에 갈 것이다.
▶ the following; the one after

779 wet [wet] 젖은

The clothes are still wet. 그 옷은 아직도 젖어 있다.
▶ covered with water

More 비교변화 wet - wetter - wettest

780 funny [fʌ́ni] 우스운, 웃기는, 재미있는

My new classmate is very friendly and funny.
나의 새로운 반 친구는 매우 친절하고 재미있다.
▶ amusing; provoking laughter

More 비교변화 funny - funnier - funniest

CHAPTER 2

UNIT 66 — Word 781~792

Shadow Speaking 332

781. care [kɛər] 돌봄, 주의
She is busy with the care of children.
그녀는 어린이들을 돌보느라 바쁘다.
▶things that are done to keep someone healthy or safe; effort made to something safely or without causing damage

782. throw [θrou] 던지다
Don't throw stones at the window. 창문에 돌을 던지지 마라.
▶to send through the air

More 동사변화 throw - threw - thrown

783. minus [máinəs] …을 뺀(제외한)
Seven minus four is three. 7 빼기 4는 3이다.
▶subtracted from; except for

784. carrot [kǽrət] 당근
Put onions and carrots first. 먼저 양파와 당근을 넣어라.
▶a type of root eaten as a vegetable and usually orange in color

785. reach [ri:tʃ] 도달하다
They will reach New York tonight.
그들은 오늘밤에 뉴욕에 도착할 할 것이다.
▶to go as far as

786. spider [spáidər] 거미
A spider is not an insect. 거미는 곤충이 아니다.
▶an animal with eight legs that builds webs

UNIT 66

787 **leader** [líːdər] 지도자, 대표

He was a great leader. 그는 위대한 지도자였다.
▶a powerful person who controls or influences what other people do

788 **tail** [teil] 꼬리

These foxes have beautiful tails.
이 여우들은 아름다운 꼬리를 가지고 있다.
▶the stick-like part of some animals which extends from their back ends

789 **friendship** [fréndʃip] 우정

Your friendship is very important to me.
너와의 우정은 나에게 매우 중요하다.
▶the state of being friends

790 **wood** [wud] 나무, 목재

All the furniture was made of wood.
모든 가구는 나무로 만들어져 있었다.
▶material that comes from trees

791 **dress** [dres] 드레스, 원피스

The woman likes a long dress. 그녀는 긴 드레스를 좋아한다.
▶a piece of clothing with a top and skirt that connect that is mainly worn by women; put on clothes

792 **donkey** [dáŋki] 당나귀

A donkey is an animal with long ears.
당나귀는 긴 귀를 가지고 있는 동물이다.
▶an animal that is part of the horse family, it is smaller than common horses

CHAPTER 2

UNIT 67 — Word 793~804

Shadow Speaking 332

듣기 134 말하기 135

793 treasure [tréʒər] 보물

That is a treasure map. 저것은 보물 지도이다.
▶ a collection of valuables

794 boil [bɔil] 끓다, 끓이다

Boil a lot of water in a pot. 냄비에 물을 많이 끓여라.
▶ to heat a liquid until it bubbles

795 insect [ínsekt] 곤충

The spider eats many insects every day.
그 거미는 매일 많은 곤충들을 먹는다.
▶ an animal with six legs, three main section of the body, and usually wings

796 camera [kǽmərə] 카메라, 사진기

I have a compact camera. 나는 소형 카메라를 가지고 있다.
▶ a device that you can use to take pictures

797 swing [swiŋ] 그네

There are two swings on the playground.
그 놀이터에는 그네가 2개 있다.
▶ a seat that hangs from a frame and lets you move up in the air and back and forth

798 medicine [médəsən] 약, 의학

The boy took his medicine. 그 소년은 그의 약을 먹었다.
▶ something that helps cure or prevents diseases

UNIT 67

799 wild [waild] 야생의

I looked at a wild rabbit. 나는 야생 토끼를 보았다.
▶ living in nature without human control or care; not tame

More 비교변화 wild - wilder - wildest, tame 길들여진

800 o'clock [əklɑk] …시(시간)

I am going to meet her at two o'clock.
나는 2시 정각에 그녀를 만날 것이다.
▶ used to express exact hours with no minutes

801 heaven [hévən] 천국

He hopes to go to heaven when he dies.
그는 그가 죽었을 때 천국에 가기를 희망한다.
▶ the place God lives

802 grasshopper [grǽshɑ̀pər] 메뚜기

We can see grasshoppers in the field.
우리는 들판에서 메뚜기를 볼 수 있다.
▶ an insect which eats plants and jumps using its back legs

803 album [ǽlbəm] 앨범

I keep the photographs in an album.
나는 사진들을 앨범에 보관한다.
▶ a book that has pages where you can keep things

804 cotton [kɑ́tn] 솜, 목화

The clothes are 100% pure cotton. 그 옷은 100퍼센트 순면이다.
▶ a soft fiber that grows around a cotton plant; material made from this

CHAPTER 2

UNIT 68 — Word 805~816

Shadow Speaking 332

듣기 136 말하기 137

805 cake [keik] 케이크

I like cakes and cookies. 나는 케이크와 쿠키를 좋아한다.
▶ a baked food made from flour, eggs, sugar, and other things

806 thief [θiːf] 도둑

He called her a thief. 그는 그녀를 도둑이라고 불렀다.
▶ a person who steals things

807 age [eidʒ] 나이, 연령

He died at the age of 70. 그는 70살에 죽었다.
▶ how old someone or something is

808 library [láibrəri] 도서관

I always go to the library. 나는 매일 도서관에 간다.
▶ a room or building used for borrowing books

809 drop [drɑp] 떨어지다, 방울

Tears dropped from her eyes. 눈물이 그녀의 눈에서 떨어졌다.
▶ to let go of something so that it falls; a very small amount of liquid that falls in a rounded shape

More drops of rain 빗방울

810 medal [médl] 메달, 훈장

She won a gold medal in the Olympics.
그녀는 올림픽에서 금메달을 땄다.
▶ a flat piece of medal that you can get by winning a sports competition or being a good soldier, etc.

UNIT 68

811 coffee [kɔ́:fi] 커피

We had apple pie and coffee for dessert.
우리는 후식으로 애플파이와 커피를 들었다.
▶ a drink that is made by mixing hot water with coffee beans

812 god [gɑd] 신, 하느님

Some people believe in God. 몇몇 사람들은 하느님을 믿는다.
▶ something seen as the creator and ruler of the universe in some religions

More goddess 여신

813 temple [témpəl] 숭배를 위한 건물(절, 사원, 신전)

Bulguksa is a beautiful and old temple.
불국사는 아름답고 오래된 절이다.
▶ a building for worship; places that people go to pay respect to who they believe in

814 below [bilóu] ~ 아래에

Write your name below the line. 이름을 줄 아래에 쓰세요.
▶ under something

More above ~ 위에

815 voice [vɔis] 목소리

I heard a woman's voice outside. 나는 밖에서 여자 목소리를 들었다.
▶ the sound made by a person

816 matter [mǽtər] 문제, 일, 물체

They had important matters to discuss.
그들은 논의해야 할 중요한 문제가 있었다.
▶ something that is being done, talked about, or thought about

Word 960 · 159

CHAPTER 2

UNIT 69 · Word 817~828

듣기 138 말하기 139

817 taste [teist] 맛, 맛을 보다
She tasted the soup. 그녀는 그 수프를 맛보았다.
▶the sweet, sour, bitter, or salty quality of a thing that you can sense when it is in your mouth; to have a particular taste

818 contest [kántest] 대회, 경기, 경연
The quiz contest is over. 그 퀴즈 대회는 끝났다.
▶an event where a winner is chosen based on some criteria

819 danger [déindʒər] 위험
We are not out of danger yet. 우리는 아직 위험에서 벗어나지 못했다.
▶a situation where someone or something may be harmed

820 save [seiv] 구하다
He saved a girl from falling into the water.
그는 한 소녀가 물에 빠지는 것을 구했다.
▶to prevent from being harmed

821 remember [rimémbər] 기억하다, 상기하다
I don't remember her phone number.
나는 그녀의 전화번호를 기억하지 못한다.
▶to think of something or someone again; to keep in mind

822 soon [suːn] 곧, 머지않아
We will get to the station soon. 우리는 곧 역에 도착할 것이다.
▶in a short time; at a time that is not long from now

UNIT 69

823 **freedom** [fríːdəm] 자유

They don't have any freedom. 그들은 자유가 전혀 없다.
▶ the state of being free

824 **believe** [bilíːv] 믿다

Columbus believed that the earth is round.
Columbus는 지구가 둥글다고 믿었다.
▶ to think that something is true; to think that what someone says is true

825 **correct** [kərékt] 올바른, 정확한

Your answers are correct. 너의 정답들이 정확하다.
▶ right; accurate; the opposite of wrong

826 **found** [faund] 설립하다

Her father founded the college in 1895.
그녀의 아버지는 1895년에 대학을 설립했다.
▶ to set up or establish

More 동사변화 found - founded - founded
동사변화(find 찾다) find - found - found

827 **dictionary** [díkʃənèri] 사전

We looked up the word in a dictionary.
우리는 그 단어를 사전에서 찾아보았다.
▶ a book that tells you what the word in a language mean

828 **village** [vílidʒ] 마을

They lived in a seaside village. 그들은 바닷가 마을에 샀다.
▶ an area with houses and other buildings that is smaller than a city; a small town

CHAPTER 2

UNIT 70

Word 829~840

Shadow Speaking 332

듣기 140 말하기 141

829 fill [fil] 채우다

He is going to fill the bottle with oil.
그는 기름으로 그 병을 채우려 한다.
▶to make something full

More be filled with(=be full of) ~으로 가득 차다

830 whose [hu:z] 누구의

Whose book is this? 이것은 누구의 책입니까?
▶question word used to ask who something belongs to

831 victory [víktəri] 승리

He is confident of victory in the finals.
그는 결승전에서 승리를 자신하고 있다.
▶a win, especially in war

832 twice [twais] 두 번

She goes to the bookstore twice a month.
그녀는 한 달에 두 번 서점에 간다.
▶two times

833 hill [hil] 언덕

We are running to the hill. 우리는 언덕으로 뛰어가고 있다.
▶a raised area of land that is smaller than a mountain

834 farmer [fá:rmər] 농부

Many farmers work in the field. 많은 농부들이 들판에서 일한다.
▶a person who grows plants for food and raises animals

UNIT 70

835 invention [invénʃən] 발명, 발명품

The Internet is a very useful invention.
인터넷은 아주 유용한 발명품이다.
▶a new creation made as a result of study and experiments

More invent 발명하다, inventor 발명가

836 taxi [tǽksi] 택시

Yesterday I came home by taxi. 어제 나는 택시로 집에 왔다.
▶a car that stops for people who pay to ride it for short trips

837 introduce [ìntrədjúːs] 소개하다

He introduced me to a pretty girl at the party.
그는 파티에서 나에게 예쁜 소녀를 소개했다.
▶to have people meet each other and tell their names to the other person or people they meet

838 wolf [wulf] 늑대

They ran after the wolf. 사람들은 그 늑대를 뒤쫓았다.
▶an animal similar to a dog that lives and hunts in groups

839 hear [hiər] 듣다

He could hear a dog barking. 그는 개가 짖는 소리를 들을 수 있었다.
▶to notice something through your ears

More 동사변화 hear - heard - heard

840 skin [skin] 피부

She has clear skin and brown eyes.
그녀는 깨끗한 피부와 갈색 눈을 지녔다.
▶the outer surface of a person's or animal's body, except for hair and feathers

CHAPTER 2

UNIT 71 — Word 841~852

Shadow Speaking 332

듣기 142 말하기 143

841 hunt [hʌnt] 사냥하다

They sometimes hunted bears in the woods.
그들은 때대로 숲에서 곰을 사냥했다.
▶to kill wild animals for food or pleasure

More hunter 사냥꾼

842 allow [əláu] 허락하다

I will allow them to play soccer in the park.
나는 그들이 공원에서 축구를 하는 것을 허락할 것이다
▶to permit someone to have or do something

843 steam [stiːm] 김, 증기

Steam rose from the boiling kettle.
끓고 있는 주전자에서 김이 올라왔다.
▶the hot gas that is created when water is boiled

844 race [reis] 경주

Who won the race? 누가 경주에서 이겼나요?
▶a competition between people, animals, vehicles, etc.

845 belong [bilɔ́(ː)ŋ] 속하다, 소유이다

This book belongs to me. 이 책은 나의 것이다.
▶to be the property of someone

846 museum [mjuːzíːəm] 박물관

He often went to the museum. 그는 가끔 박물관에 갔다.
▶a building in which interesting and valuable things are collected and shown to the public

UNIT 71

847 **favorite** [féivərit] 가장 좋아하는

My favorite color is blue. 내가 가장 좋아하는 색깔은 파란색이다.
▶most liked

848 **collect** [kəlékt] 모으다, 수집하다

I collected stamps and postcards. 나는 우표와 엽서를 모았다.
▶to get things from different places and bring them together

More collection 수집

849 **excellent** [éksələnt] 우수한, 탁월한

He is excellent in English composition.
그는 영어 영작 실력이 우수하다.
▶very good

More 비교변화 excellent - more excellent - most excellent

850 **theater** [θí(:)ətər] 극장

There is a movie theater near my house.
나의 집 근처에 영화 극장이 있다.
▶a building where plays and shows are performed

851 **fashion** [fǽʃən] 유행, 인기

Jeans are still in fashion. 청바지는 여전히 인기가 있다.
▶a popular way of dressing during a particular time or among a particular group of people

852 **popular** [pápjələr] 있기 있는

This is one of our most popular designs.
이것은 가장 인기 있는 디자인 중에 하나이다.
▶liked or enjoyed by many people

More 비교변화 popular - more popular - most popular

CHAPTER 2

UNIT 72 — Word 853~864

Shadow Speaking 332

듣기 144 말하기 145

853 culture [kʌ́ltʃər] 문화
Seoul is a city full of culture and history.
서울은 문화와 역사가 가득한 도시이다.
▶ the beliefs, customs, arts, etc., of a particular society, group, place, or time

854 lot [lɑt] 많음, 다량
She still has a lot to learn. 그녀는 여전히 배울 게 많다.
▶ a large amount

855 power [páuər] 힘, 권력
Knowledge is power. 지식은 힘이다.
▶ the ability or right to control people or things

856 quite [kwait] 꽤, 상당히
My brother plays quite well. 나의 남동생은 운동을 꽤 잘한다.
▶ very; to a very noticeable degree or extent

857 law [lɔː] 법
The king's word is law in the country.
그 나라에서 그 왕의 말은 법이다.
▶ the rules made by the government of a country

858 foreign [fɔ́(ː)rin] 외국의
I traveled to a lot of foreign countries.
나는 외국의 많은 나라를 여행했다.
▶ located outside a particular place or country

UNIT 72

859 different [dífərənt] 다른

The goods were different from the sample.
그 상품은 그 견본과 달랐다.
▶not of the same quality

More difference 차이

860 guess [ges] 추측하다

We only guess at her reasons for leaving.
우리는 그녀가 떠난 이유를 추측할 뿐이다.
▶to give an answer about something when you do not know much or anything about it

861 angel [éindʒəl] 천사

She looks like an angel. 그녀는 천사처럼 보인다.
▶a spiritual being that serves especially as a messenger from God or as a guardian of human beings

862 boring [bɔ́ːriŋ] 지루한

That is a very boring book. 저것은 매우 지루한 책이다.
▶dull and uninteresting

More 비교변화 boring - more boring - most boring

863 promise [prάmis] 약속

She kept her promise to visit there.
그녀는 거기에 방문하겠다는 약속을 지켰다.
▶a statement telling someone that you will definitely do something or that something will definitely happen

864 unhappy [ʌnhǽpi] 불행한, 슬픈, 우울한

He looked unhappy yesterday. 그녀는 어제 슬퍼 보였다.
▶not happy; sad or depressed

More 비교변화 unhappy - unhappier - unhappiest

Word 960 • 167

CHAPTER 2

UNIT 73 — Word 865~876

Shadow Speaking 332

865 health [helθ] 건강
Early rising is good for the health. 일찍 일어나는 것은 건강에 좋다.
▶ the condition of being well or free from disease

866 delicious [dilíʃəs] 맛있는
The beef steak tasted delicious. 그 소고기 스테이크는 맛있었다.
▶ very pleasant to taste

More 비교변화 delicious - more delicious - most delicious

867 energy [énərdʒi] 정력, 활기
The children are always full of energy.
그 어린이들은 항상 활기가 넘친다.
▶ ability to be active

868 touch [tʌtʃ] 만지다
He touched it with his umbrella.
그는 그것에 그의 우산을 대어 보았다.
▶ to put your hand or fingers on someone or something

869 join [dʒɔin] 합류하다
Will you join us for lunch? 우리랑 점심 같이 할래요?
▶ to go somewhere in order to be with

870 special [spéʃəl] 특별한
There is something special about this place.
이 장소에는 뭔가 특별한 점이 있다.
▶ different from what is normal or usual

UNIT 73

871 science [sáiəns] 과학

My favorite subject is science. 내가 가장 좋아하는 과목은 과학이다.
▶ study of the natural world based on facts learned through experiments and observation

872 perfect [pə́ːrfikt] 완벽한

She speaks perfect English. 그녀는 완벽한 영어를 구사한다.
▶ having no mistakes or flaws

More 비교변화 perfect - more perfect - most perfect

873 simple [símpəl] 간단한, 단순한

This machine is very simple to use.
이 기계는 사용하는 게 매우 간단하다.
▶ not hard to understand or do

More 비교변화 simple - simpler - simplest

874 difference [dífərəns] 차이

There is no difference in the results of the test.
그 시험 성적에는 차이가 없다.
▶ the quality that makes one person or thing unlike another

875 picnic [píknik] 소풍

I went on a picnic beside the river. 나는 강가로 소풍을 갔다.
▶ a trip or party that includes a meal eaten outdoors

876 mistake [mistéik] 실수, 오해하다

We all make mistakes. 우리 모두는 실수를 한다.
▶ something that is not correct; to understand something or someone incorrectly

More 동사변화 mistake - mistook - mistaken

CHAPTER 2

UNIT 74 — Word 877~888

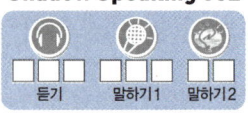

---

877 neighbor [néibər] 이웃, 이웃사람

My neighbor helped me fix my bike.
나의 이웃이 나의 자전거 고치는 것을 도와주었다.
▶ a person who lives next to or near another person

878 information [ìnfərméiʃən] 정보

A dictionary gives information about words.
사전은 어휘에 대한 정보를 준다.
▶ facts or details about a subject

879 succeed [səksíːd] 성공하다

My uncle succeeded in business. 나의 삼촌은 사업에 성공했다.
▶ to achieve the desired result

More success 성공, succeed in ~에 성공하다

880 main [mein] 주된, 중요한

The main thing is to study hard every day.
중요한 것은 매일 열심히 공부하는 것이다.
▶ most important

881 honest [ánist] 정직한

She is a kind and honest girl. 그녀는 친절하고 정직한 소녀이다.
▶ good and truthful

More 비교변화 honest - more honest - most honest

882 exam [igzǽm] 시험

I got my exam results today. 난 오늘 시험 결과를 받았다.
▶ a test to show a person's progress, knowledge, or ability

UNIT 74

883　waste [weist] 낭비, 쓰레기, 낭비하다

We must find ways to reduce unnecessary waste.
우리는 불필요한 낭비를 줄일 방법을 찾아야 한다.
▶something you throw away; to use in a way that is not necessary or effective

884　abroad [əbrɔ́ːd] 해외에서, 해외로

She worked abroad for a year. 그녀는 일 년 동안 해외에서 근무했다.
▶to a foreign country

885　difficult [dífikʌ̀lt] 어려운

The task is difficult for me. 그 일은 내게는 힘이 든다.
▶not easy

More　비교변화 difficult - more difficult - most difficult

886　education [édʒukèiʃən] 교육

Home education is as important as school education.
가정교육은 학교교육만큼이나 중요하다.
▶the process of teaching someone especially in a school

More　educate 교육하다

887　sharp [ʃaːrp] 날카로운

He has a small sharp knife. 그는 작고 날카로운 칼이 있다.
▶having a fine point that is able to make a hole in things

More　비교변화 sharp - sharper - sharpest

888　instead [instéd] 대신에

My sister was sick so I went instead.
나의 여동생이 아파서 나는 대신 갔다.
▶in place of; rather than

CHAPTER 2

UNIT 75

Word 889~900

Shadow Speaking 332

듣기 150 말하기 151

889 plus [plʌs] …을 더하기여, 플러스

Two plus five is seven. 2 더하기 5는 7이다.
▶added to; in addition (to)

890 feel [fiːl] 느끼다

I felt my heart beat violently.
나는 나의 심장이 격렬하게 뛰는 것을 느꼈다.
▶to be aware of something that affects you physically

More 동사변화 feel - felt -felt

891 pair [pɛər] 한 쌍, 한 벌

I bought a pair of socks. 나는 양말 한 켤레를 샀다.
▶two things that are same and are made to be used together

892 achieve [ətʃíːv] 달성하다, 성취하다

He had finally achieved success. 그는 마침내 성공을 거두었다.
▶to get something by working hard

More achievement 달성, 성취

893 finally [fáinəli] 마침내

The performance finally started an hour late.
그 공연은 마침내 1시간 반 늦게 시작되었다.
▶in the end

894 discover [diskʌ́vər] 발견하다, 알다

I discovered him to be a liar. 나는 그가 거짓말쟁이인 것을 알았다.
▶to see, find, or become aware of something for the first time

UNIT 75

895 roof [ru:f, ruf] 지붕

Tim climbed on to the garage roof. Tim이 차고 지붕으로 올라갔다.
▶ the top cover of a house

More 복수형 roofs

896 crazy [kréizi] 정상이 아닌

She is pretty but too crazy. 그녀는 예쁘지만 매우 정상이 아니다.
▶ very strange; not of right mind

More 비교변화 crazy - crazier - craziest

897 straw [strɔː] 짚, 밀짚, 빨대

The man is drinking with a straw.
그 남자는 빨대를 이용해 마시고 있다.
▶ the dry stems of wheat and other grain plants; a thin tube used for sucking up a drink

898 raise [reiz] 올리다, 기르다

I was born and raised a city boy. 나는 도시 소년으로 나고 자랐다.
▶ to lift or move to a higher position; to take care of something or someone until adulthood

899 rescue [réskjuː] 구조하다

He rescued a child from an embarrassing situation.
그는 어린이를 난처한 상황에서 구했다.
▶ to prevent from being harmed

900 return [ritə́ːrn] 돌아오다, 돌아가다

I waited a long time for him to return.
나는 그가 돌아오기를 오랜 시간 기다렸다.
▶ to go back to a place

CHAPTER 2

UNIT 76 — Word 901~912

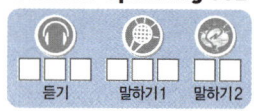

듣기 152 말하기 153

901 nature [néitʃər] 자연

Nature is the best doctor. 자연은 가장 좋은 의사이다.
▶ the physical world and everything in it that is not made by people

902 usual [júːʒuəl] 보통의, 평상시의

He came home later than usual. 그는 평상시보다 더 늦게 귀가했다.
▶ as is done most of the time

903 almost [ɔ́ːlmoust] 거의

Their house is almost opposite ours.
그들의 집은 우리 집 거의 맞은편이다.
▶ nearly; said of actions almost completed, but not quite

904 fry [frai] 굽다, 튀기다

Don't fry the cheese too long. 치즈를 오랫동안 굽지 마라.
▶ to cook something by heating it on or in oil

905 machine [məʃíːn] 기계

How does this machine work? 이 기계는 어떻게 작동되나요?
▶ an object that used energy to perform a task

906 possible [pásəbəl] 가능한

We spent every possible moment on the beach.
우리는 가능한 모든 순간을 해변에서 보냈다.
▶ capable of happening

UNIT 76

907 **lose** [luːz] 잃어버리다, 분실하다

She lost her bag in the crowd.
그녀는 사람들 속에서 그녀의 가방을 잃어버렸다.
▶to be unable to find somthing or someone

More 동사변화 lose - lost - lost

908 **last** [læst] 마지막의, 계속되다

They caught the last train home.
그들은 집으로 가는 마지막 기차를 탔다.
▶coming after all other in time, order, or imfortance; to continue in time

909 **break** [breik] 깨다, 부수다

He broke the chocolate in two. 그가 초콜릿을 2조각으로 부러뜨렸다.
▶to separate into parts or pieces often in a sudden and forceful

More 동사변화 break - broke - broken

910 **favor** [féivər] 취향, 부탁

I have a favor to ask you. 나는 당신에게 한 가지 부탁이 있다.
▶an act of kindness; an act done for the benefit of another

911 **wave** [weiv] 파도

Children were playing in the waves.
아이들이 파도 속에서 놀고 있었다.
▶a moving mountain of water

912 **enemy** [énəmi] 적

Yesterday our soldiers attacked the enemy.
어제 우리 병사들이 적을 공격했다.
▶one who opposes another; a person one hates

CHAPTER 2

UNIT 77 Word 913~924

---

913 truck [trʌk] 트럭

John wants to be a truck driver. John은 트럭 운전기가 되고 싶어한다.
▶ a big car that has four or more wheels that is used for carrying large things

914 brick [brik] 벽돌

The school is built of brick. 그 학교는 벽돌로 지어져 있다.
▶ a hard material made from clay used for building things

915 mean [miːn] 의미하다

What does this word mean? 이 단어는 무슨 뜻인가요?
▶ to intend to express

916 gallery [gǽləri] 화랑, 미술관

I will go to the gallery next weekend.
나는 다음 주말에 미술관에 갈 것이다.
▶ a building in which people look at paintings

917 service [sə́ːrvis] 봉사, 서비스

The food was good but the service was very low.
음식은 좋았지만 서비스 수준은 아주 낮았다.
▶ work done to help others

918 mix [miks] 섞다

Oil doesn't mix with water. 기름은 물과 섞이지 않는다.
▶ to combine into one mass

UNIT 77

919 baseball [béisbɔ̀ːl] 야구

I played baseball with my classmates.
나는 반 친구들과 야구를 했다.
▶ a game played on a large field by two teams of nine players

920 sorrow [sárou] 슬픔, 비애

He expressed his sorrow at the news of her death.
그는 그녀의 사망 소식에 큰 슬픔을 표했다.
▶ a deep sadness

921 lock [lɑk] 잠그다

He carefully locked the door behind him.
그는 그 뒤에서 조심스럽게 그 문을 잠갔다.
▶ to close using a lock; to close with an object requiring a key to open

922 distance [dístəns] 거리

They had to walk a short distance to the hotel.
호텔까지 조금 걷지 않으면 안 되었다.
▶ a measurement between two points

923 area [ɛ́əriə] 지역, 면적

She knows the desert area very well.
그녀는 그 사막 지역을 아주 잘 알고 있다.
▶ a part or section within a larger place; a measurement found by multiplying the length and the height

924 shocked [ʃɑːkt] 충격을 받은

At first I was really shocked. 처음에 나는 충격을 받았다.
▶ surprised by some news

More shock 충격, 충격을 주다

CHAPTER 2

UNIT 78

Word 925~936

Shadow Speaking 332

듣기 156 말하기 157

925 melt [melt] 녹다
Both sugar and salt melt in water. 설탕이나 소금 모두 물에 녹는다.
▶ to change from a solid to a liquid usually because of heat

926 speech [spi:tʃ] 연설, 말하기 능력
She won the English speech contest.
그는 영어 말하기 대회에서 우승했다.
▶ a talk about a certain subject

927 rule [ru:l] 규칙, 원칙
There is no rule without some exceptions.
예외 없는 규칙은 없다. (속담)
▶ law; code of conduct

928 hunter [hʌ́ntər] 사냥꾼
The hunter found a big tiger in the mountain.
그 사냥꾼은 그 산에서 큰 호랑이를 발견했다.
▶ a person who hunts

929 chance [tʃæns] 기회
Please give me a chance to explain. 제게 설명할 기회를 주세요.
▶ possibility for someone to do or have something

930 forward [fɔ́:rwərd] 앞으로
He took two steps forward. 그가 앞으로 두 걸음을 뗐다.
▶ toward the front

UNIT 78

931 shadow [ʃǽdou] 그림자

The children were following each other's shadows.
그 아이들은 각자의 그림자를 따라다니고 있다.
▶ a dark area caused by something blocking light

932 practice [præktis] 연습하다, 실습하다, 연습

The team is practicing for their game on Sunday.
그 팀은 일요일에 있을 그들의 게임을 위해 연습하고 있다.
▶ to do something over again learn it; the activity of doing somthing again to become better at it

933 curtain [kə́:rtən] 커튼

The curtains were still closed. 커튼은 여전히 쳐져 있었다.
▶ a sheet of cloth that hangs from a bar above a window and is used to cover it

934 important [impɔ́:rtənt] 중요한

She is an important part of the team.
그녀는 그 팀에서 중요한 역할을 하고 있다.
▶ significant; having serious meaning or worth

More 비교변화 important - more important - most important, importance 중요

935 chef [ʃef] 요리사

Her ambition is to become a chef.
그녀의 목표는 요리사가 되는 것이다.
▶ a professional cook at a restaurant

936 challenge [tʃǽlindʒ] 도전하다

Mike challenged me to a game of chess.
Mike는 체스를 한 판 두고 나에게 도전해 왔다.
▶ to call to engage in a contest or fight

CHAPTER 2

UNIT 79

Word 937~948

듣기 158 말하기 159

937 agree [əgríː] 동의하다

When she said that, we had to agree.
그녀가 그 말을 했을 때 우리는 동의해야 했다.
▶to accept a proposition; to concur with a statement

938 origin [ɔ́ːrədʒin] 기원, 근원

What is the origin of that word? 그 단어의 기원은 무엇인가요?
▶the point or place where something begins or is created

939 divide [diváid] 나누다

We divided the work between us. 우리는 그 일을 우리끼리 나누었다.
▶to decrease by division

940 surprised [sərpráizd] 놀란

I was surprised to hear of the news. 나는 그 소식을 듣고 놀랐다.
▶having the feeling that people get when somthing unexpected; feeling surprise

941 gift [gift] 선물

The watch was a gift from my father.
그 시계는 우리 아버지께서 주신 선물이었다.
▶present; something that is given to another person

942 artist [áːrtist] 예술가, 화가

She will be a great artist. 그녀는 위대한 화가가 될 것이다.
▶a person who makes art

UNIT 79

943 cage [keidʒ] 우리, 새장

The bird escaped from its cage. 그 새는 우리에서 도망쳤다.
▶a kind of box made with wires or metal bars in which an animal is kept

944 bright [brait] 밝은, 빛나는

The lighting was too bright. 그 불빛은 매우 밝았다.
▶having a strong light; smart

More 비교변화 bright - brighter - brightest

945 experiment [ikspérəmənt] 실험, 실험하다

The scientist is planning a new experiment.
그 과학자는 새로운 실험을 계획하고 있다.
▶a scientific or academic test; to make experiment

946 adventure [ədvéntʃər] 모험

He told us about his adventures.
그는 우리에게 그의 모험에 대해 이야기를 했다.
▶a dangerous or risky activity with lots of excitement

947 painting [péintiŋ] 그림

There are many paintings in the cave.
그 동굴 안에는 많은 그림이 있다.
▶a picture made using paint

948 company [kʌ́mpəni] 회사

His father worked for a big company.
그의 아버지는 큰 회사에서 근무했다.
▶a business organization that makes or sells goods in exchange for money

CHAPTER 2

UNIT 80

Word 949~960

---

949 arrow [ǽrou] 화살

The people used bows and arrows for hunting.
그 사람들은 사냥을 위해 활과 화살을 이용했다.
▶a stick with a sharp end that is shot with a bow

950 view [vju:] 경치, 전망, 시야

The sun disappeared from view. 해가 시야에서 사라졌다
▶the things that can be seen from a particular place

951 among [əmʌ́ŋ] ~ 중에, ~에 둘러싸인

She was sitting among the boys. 그녀는 그 소년들 사이에 앉아 있었다.
▶in the presence of; surrounded by

952 excited [iksáitid] 신이 난, 흥분한

The children were excited about opening their presents.
그 아이들은 선물을 열어 보느라 신이 나 있었다.
▶very enthusiastic and eager about something

953 lend [lend] 빌려주다

Can you lend me your car this evening?
오늘 저녁에 자네 차 좀 빌려 줄 수 있겠나?
▶to let someone use something temporarily

954 beat [bi:t] 때리다, 두드리다

Someone was beating a drum. 누군가가 북을 치고 있었다.
▶to hit violently

More 동사변화 beat - beat - beat

UNIT 80

955 enough [inʌ́f] 필요한 만큼의, 충분히

There was food enough for all.
모두가 먹을 수 있을 만큼의 음식이 있었다.
▶ as much as is needed; sufficiently

956 cucumber [kjúːkəmbər] 오이

Mom cut the cucumber thinly.
엄마는 오이를 얇게 썰었다.
▶ a long, round green fruit, usually eaten as a vegetable

More eggplant 가지, carrot 당근, cabbage 양배추, onion 양파

957 several [sévərəl] 몇몇의

Several letters arrived this morning.
몇 통의 편지가 오늘 오전에 도착했다.
▶ a number more than 2 or 3 but not many

958 still [stil] 여전히, 아직(도)

Do you still live at the same address?
당신은 아직 같은 주소에 사세요?
▶ until now; happening or existing before now and continuing into the present

959 actor [ǽktər] 남자 배우

I decided to be an actor when I was fifteen.
나는 15살 때 배우가 되기로 결심했어요.
▶ a person who acts in a play, movie, etc.

More actress 여자 배우

960 job [dʒɑb] 일, 직업

He took a job as a chef. 그는 요리사로 취직했다.
▶ a task that someone has; the work that a person does regularly to earn money

Spelling Bee 100

⭐ **[1-30]** 단어의 의미를 읽고, 알맞은 단어를 쓰세요. (Unit 51-60)

1. _____ : a piece of paper that enables you to get into the theatre and watch the movie

2. _____ : a forest; an area with many trees

3. _____ : an instrument with a skin stretched over the frame

4. _____ : to take something without permission

5. _____ : the study of numbers, shapes and logic

6. _____ : two people who look exactly the same; two people who share the same DNA

7. _____ : a large area of water surrounded by land

8. _____ : not living; not alive

9. _____ : the part of your body that pumps blood

10. _____ : a furry animal that is usually brown with four hooved legs and horns on the male

11. _____ : something that is not true; to tell a lie

12. _____ : to come into sight; to become visible

13. _____ : the soul of a dead person which is visible to living people

14. _____ : well known by many people

15. _____ : something that you give to someone: the current time

16. _____ : a long, hard seat that can hold a few people

17. _____ : to make clear or easy to understand

18. _____ : someone who needs medical care

19. _____ : to excuse a past wrong

20. _____ : something that is true

21. _____ : a light flying object tied to a string which a person holds on the ground

22. _____ : to have an angry disagreement about something

23. _____ : flames that come from something burning

24. _____ : a person whose job is to protect a country, often by fighting

25. _____ : the solid surface of the earth

26. _____ : a solid yellowish food that is made from the cream of milk

27. _____ : showing intelligence or skill

28. _____ : the thing which covers birds and no other animal

29. _____ : a man who delivers mail

30. _____ : the son of a king and queen

Spelling Bee 100

⭐ **[31-60]** 단어의 의미를 읽고, 알맞은 단어를 쓰세요. (Unit 61-70)

31. _____ : full of wisdom

32. _____ : the sandy land along a sea or ocean

33. _____ : the month and day that one was born

34. _____ : to make a decision

35. _____ : to have an intention to do something; to make details for a course of action

36. _____ : the hard, white parts of the body that make up the skeleton

37. _____ : to give a penalty to

38. _____ : something that the ears can hear

39. _____ : a kind of large house or mansion used by a leader of a nation

40. _____ : frozen water

41. _____ : to go from one place to another

42. _____ : a student in the same class as another

43. _____ : covered with water

44. _____ : an animal with eight legs that builds webs

45. _____ : material that comes from trees

46. _____ : to heat a liquid until it bubbles

47. _____ : a device that you can use to take pictures

48. _____ : living in nature without human control or care; not tame

49. _____ : a book that has pages where you can keep things

50. _____ : a person who steals things

51. _____ : a room or building used for borrowing books

52. _____ : the sound made by a person

53. _____ : something that is being done, talked about, or thought about

54. _____ : a situation where someone or something may be harmed

55. _____ : to prevent from being harmed

56. _____ : the state of being free

57. _____ : a book that tells you what the word in a language mean

58. _____ : to make something full

59. _____ : a raised area of land that is smaller than a mountain

60. _____ : the outer surface of a person's or animal's body, except for hair and feathers

Spelling Bee 100

[61-100] 단어의 의미를 읽고, 알맞은 단어를 쓰세요. (Unit71-80)

61. _____ : to kill wild animals for food or pleasure

62. _____ : a building where plays and shows are performed

63. _____ : located outside a particular or country

64. _____ : something that is not correct; to understand something or someone incorrectly

65. _____ : the hot gas that is created when water is boiled

66. _____ : a building in which interesting and valuable things are collected and shown to the public

67. _____ : to get things from different places and bring them together

68. _____ : liked or enjoyed by many people

69. _____ : the ability or right to control people or things

70. _____ : the rules made by the government of a country

71. _____ : a spiritual being that serves especially as a messenger from God or as a guardian of human beings

72. _____ : dull and uninteresting

73. _____ : the condition of being well or free from disease

74. _____ : to put your hand or fingers on someone or something

75. _____ : different from what is normal or usual
76. _____ : study of the natural world based on facts learned through experiments and observation
77. _____ : a person who lives next to or near another person
78. _____ : to achieve the desired result
79. _____ : a test to show a person's progress, knowledge, or ability
80. _____ : the process of teaching someone especially in a school
81. _____ : be aware of something that affects you physically
82. _____ : to see, find, or become aware of something for the first time
83. _____ : the dry stems of wheat and other grain plants; a thin tube used for sucking up a drink
84. _____ : to lift or move to a higher position; to take care of something or someone until adulthood
85. _____ : the physical world and everything in it that is not made by people
86. _____ : an object that used energy to perform a task
87. _____ : to separate into parts or pieces often in a sudden and forceful
88. _____ : a moving mountain of water

Spelling Bee 100

89. _____ : a hard material made from clay used for building things

90. _____ : to combine into one mass

91. _____ : to close using a lock; to close with an object requiring a key to open

92. _____ : a part or section within a larger place; a measurement found by multiplying the length and the height

93. _____ : to change from a solid to a liquid usually because of heat

94. _____ : possibility for someone to do or have something

95. _____ : a dark area caused by something blocking light

96. _____ : the point or place where something begins or is created

97. _____ : a kind of box made with wires or metal bars in which an animal is kept

98. _____ : a business organization that makes or sells goods in exchange for money

99. _____ : the things that can be seen from a particular place

100. _____ : a task that someone has; the work that a person does regularly to earn money

Appendix

초등 영단어 960은 영어 단어장이 아닙니다.
Shadow Speaking 332학습을 기반으로 영단어를 통해
영어를 익히도록 설계된 신개념 학습법입니다.

1. Key Word 240 (중등 빈도수 높은 단어)

2. Word List 960 (초등 영단어 960 색인)

3. Weekly Test 총16회 (5개 Unit마다 1회 제공)

4. Answers (Spelling Bee)

부록 1 Key Word 240 (중등 빈도수 높은 영단어)

1. **above** [əbʌ́v] – in a higher place ~보다 위에(위로)

2. **accept** [æksépt] – to receive willingly 받아들이다

3. **add** [æd] – to increase by addition; to find the sum of two or more numbers 더하다, 추가하다, 합계를 내다

4. **admire** [ædmáiər] – to respect or esteem; to hold in high regard 감탄하다, 존경하다

5. **alike** [əláik] – similar in appearance, nature, or form 비슷한

6. **alive** [əláiv] – living; not dead 살아있는

7. **along** [əlɔ́:ŋ] – next to the length of something ~을 따라

8. **amount** [əmáunt] – sum; a quantity of something 총계, 양

9. **announce** [ənáuns] – to say publicly 발표하다

10. **anything** [éniθiŋ] – a thing of any kind 아무것, 무엇이든

11. **anywhere** [énihwɛ̀ər] – in any place 어디에(서도)

12. **approach** [əpróutʃ] – to go or come near 다가가다

13. **argument** [á:rgjəmənt] – a dispute; a fight with word 논의, 논쟁, 말다툼

14. **armor** [á:rmər] – a protective covering used in fighting 갑옷

15. **arrest** [ərést] – to take to jail or prison 체포하다

16. **awake** [əwéik] – conscious; not asleep 깨어있는, 잠들지 않은

17. **bang** [bæg] – to hit hard to make noise 쾅하고 치다

18. **base** [beis] – the part of something that provides support for the rest of it; bottom 기초, 바탕, 맨 아래 부분

19. battle [bǽtl] – a large fight; one of the fights of a war 싸움

20. bead [biːd] – a small ball with a hole through it, often used for jewelry 구슬

21. beg [beg] – to ask for something for free; to request urgently or often 구걸하다, 간청하다

22. betray [bitréi] – to give information about a person to an enemy 정보를 넘겨 주다

23. bite [bait] – to cut into or through something using one's teeth 물다

24. blood [blʌd] – a liquid that carries oxygen throughout our bodies 피

25. bloom [bluːm] – to open when ripe; to become ripe 꽃이 피다

26. bravery [bréivəri] – the quality or state of being brave 용기

27. breathe [briːð] – to take in air through the nose or mouth 숨을 쉬다

28. brook [bruk] – a stream of water smaller than a river 개울, 시내

29. burn [bəːrn] – to consume fuel and make heat, light and, gases 태우다

30. bury [béri] – to place something in the ground and cover it with dirt 묻다

31. calculate [kǽlkjəlèit] – to find an answer by using math 계산하다

32. carriage [kǽridʒ] – a vehicle with wheels that is pulled by a horse 마차

33. case [keis] – a situation that is an instance or example of something; a container for keeping or carrying things 경우, 상자나 용기

34. castle [kǽsl] – a large building usually with high, thick walls and towers 성, 성곽

35. cause [kɔːz] – to make happen 발생하다

Key Word 240

36. cave [keiv] − a hole in a rock or the ground that is big enough for a person to enter 동굴

37. ceiling [síːliŋ] − the top side of a room 천장

38. charm [tʃɑːrm] − a kind of jewelry that brings good luck 매력

39. chase [tʃeis] − to follow quickly and try to catch someone or something 쫓다

40. cheer [tʃiər] − to yell or chant excitedly in favor of someone or a team 격려하다

41. choke [tʃouk] − to die from not being able to breathe 질식시키다

42. chop [tʃɑp] − to cut into pieces (도끼로) 자르다

43. clue [kluː] − hint; something that helps one learn the truth 실마리, 단서

44. complicated [kɑ́mpləkèitid] − complex; difficult; hard to understand or explain 복잡한, 까다로운, 알기 어려운

45. cone [koun] − a circular object that decreases to a point at one end, giving it a triangular appearance 원뿔

46. confused [kənfjúːzd] − having difficulty to understand 혼란한, 당황한

47. consider [kənsídər] − to think about carefully 숙고하다, 고려하다

48. continue [kəntínjuː] − to do something without stopping; to keep doing something 계속하다

49. course [kɔːrs] − a set group of lessons coming one after another for the purpose of teaching a subject 진로, 과정

50. crack [kræk] − a break only on the surface of something 갈라진 금

51. crawl [krɔːl] − to move on one's hands and knees 기다

52. cream [kri:m] – the fatty part of milk that rises to its surface 크림

53. cricket [kríkit] – a small insect which moves by jumping, male crickets makenoise by rubbing their wings together 귀뚜라미

54. criminal [krímənəl] – someone who commits a crime; for example, a thief or murderer 범죄자

55. crop [krɑp] – the food obtained from plants 농작물

56. curious [kjúəriəs] – filled with wonder 신기한

57. current [kə́:rənt] – a continuous movement of water or air 흐름

58. dawn [dɔ:n] – the time of day when the sun first comes up 새벽

59. deaf [def] – not being able to hear 귀머거리의

60. demand [dimǽnd] – to order; to request forcefully 요구하다

61. dial [dáiəl] – to press a phone number into a phone 전화를 걸다

62. disappear [dìsəpíər] – to cease to be visible 사라지다

63. disciple [disáipəl] – a person who believes and helps spread the teachings of another person 제자

64. disguise [disgáiz] – to hide one's true appearance 위장하다

65. duel [djú:əl] – an planned fight between two people done for honor 결투

66. duke [dju:k] – a british peer of the highest rank 공작

67. dumb [dʌm] – not being able to speak; mute 벙어리의

68. dying [dying] – in the process of dying; ending of life 죽어가는

69. engineer [éndʒəníər] – a person who designs and builds complicated products or machines 기술자

Key Word 240

70. envelope [énvəlòup] – a folded paper used to hold letters or other items to mail 봉투

71. escape [iskéip] – to get away from; to avoid something bad 달아나다, 탈출하다

72. everything [évriθiŋ] – all things; each thing 모든 것

73. examine [igzǽmin] – to look at carefully in search of information 검사하다

74. excite [iksáit] – to get one very interested in something 흥분시키다

75. explorer [iksplɔ́:rər] – someone who travels to new places to find new things 모험가

76. faint [feint] – suddenly lose consciousness 실신한

77. fair [fɛər] – being right and reasonable in the way things are dealt with; carnival; a traveling show 공평한, 축제, 박람회

78. fear [fiər] – emotion of being afraid 두려움, 공포

79. fix [fiks] – to change something so that it works correctly 고치다

80. flap [flæp] – to move up and down (wings) 퍼덕거리다

81. flood [flʌd] – a large amount of water covering an area of land 홍수

82. flour [flauər] – a finely milled wheat, often used for making bread and similar foods 밀가루

83. frown [fraun] – to make an expression of dislike by using the face 얼굴을 찡그리다

84. gardener [gá:rdnər] – a person who works in a garden 정원사

85. grab [græb] – to take or seize suddenly with the hand 잡다

86. grain [grein] – a seed or fruit of a cereal grass 낟알, 곡물

87. grateful [gréitfəl] – with thanks 고마워하는

88. grave [greiv] – a place where a dead person is buried 묘지

89. handle [hǽndl] – to touch, feel, hold, or move (something) with your hand 다루다

90. height [hait] – the length from bottom to top 키, 높이

91. hire [háiər] – to pay someone to work regularly for oneself or a business 고용하다

92. horrible [hɔ́:rəbəl] – terrible; very bad or unpleasant 무서운, 끔직한

93. hose [houz] – a long, flexible tube that carries water from another place 호스

94. hug [hʌg] – to put one's arms around another person to show love or affection 꼭 껴안다

95. intend [inténd] – to have in mind as a purpose or goal ~할 작정이다

96. iron [áiərn] – a kind of metal that is silver-white in color; a device with a flat metal base that is heated and is used to press wrinkles out of clothing 철, 다리미

97. jealous [dʒéləs] – envious; wanting what someone else has 질투심이 많은

98. junk [dʒʌŋk] – garbage; useless things 쓰레기, 잡동사니

99. lampshade [lǽmpʃèid] – a covering that used to hide a light bulb from being seen 램프갓

100. language [lǽŋgwidʒ] – a system of sounds and meanings used to communicate 언어

Key Word 240

101. *later* [léitər] – at a future time; at a time following 뒤에, 나중에

102. *lead* [li:d] – to show the way to others 이끌다

103. *length* [leŋkθ] – the longest distance from one side to the other of an object 길이

104. *lens* [lenz] – a glass which bends light 렌즈

105. *leopard* [lépərd] – a large strong cat living in asia and africa that has black spots on its body 표범

106. *lip* [lip] – the two fleshy parts that stick out in front of your teeth 입술

107. *list* [list] – a group of things in the same category written one after another 목록, 명단

108. *lunar* [lú:nər] – of or relating to the moon 달의, 음력의

109. *magnet* [mǽgnit] – something that attracts, usually metals 자석

110. *maid* [meid] – a woman who does housework for another person 하녀

112. *mark* [ma:rk] – to make a sign to show where something is ~에 표시를 하다

113. *marriage* [mǽridʒ] – the state of being married; the action of getting married 결혼

114. *master* [mǽstər] – a person who is very skilled in something 장인, 달인

115. *mathematician* [mæ̀θəmətíʃən] – a person who is an expert in mathematics 수학자

116. *maze* [meiz] – a group of complex paths in which one can easily become lost 미로

117. *measure* [méʒər] – to determine the length or size of 측정하다

118. *merchant* [mə́:rtʃənt] – a person who buys and sells goods 상인

119. **meter** [míːtər] − a length that is equal to 100cm 미터

120. **mine** [main] − a tunnel from which minerals are taken 광산

121. **minister** [mínistər] − a person with a high government position 장관, 대신

122. **miser** [máizər] − a rich person who doesn't use their money 구두쇠

123. **mole** [moul] − a small, furry animal that lives in the ground and eat small animals such as worms 두더지

124. **monk** [mʌŋk] − a religious man who devotes himself to religion and lives in a special building with other monks 승려

125. **mosquito** [məskíːtou] − a small flying insect, female mosquitoes suck blood from humans and animals 모기

126. **multiply** [mʌ́ltəplài] − to increase by multiplication 늘리다, 곱하다

127. **mustache** [mʌ́stæʃ] − hair on one's upper lip 콧수염

128. **narrow** [nívər] − being small in width 좁은

129. **nervous** [nə́ːrvəs] − uneasy; worried 신경질적인, 불안한

130. **nobody** [nóubàdi] − not one person; no person 아무도 ~않은

131. **nothing** [nʌ́θiŋ] − not any thing; not one thing 아무것도 ~않은

132. **own** [oun] − belonging to oneself or itself 자기 자신의

133. **painful** [péinfəl] − hurtful; causing pain 아픈

134. **path** [pæθ] − a small, dirt road 길, 작은 길

135. **pauper** [pɔ́ːpər] − a very poor person 거지

136. **peck** [pek] − to hit something with one's beak, often repeatedly, usually used when speaking of birds (부리로) 쪼다

Key Word 240

137. permit [pəːrmít] – to allow; to let happen 허락하다

138. pity [píti] – a feeling of sorrow for another 동정

139. plug [plʌg] – to fill a hole to stop things from entering or leaving 마개를 하다

140. portrait [pɔ́ːrtrit] – a picture of a person 초상화

141. poster [póustər] – a piece of paper with Word or pictures that you can hang on a wall 포스터, 벽보

142. pot [pɑt] – a round metal container with high sides used for cooking 단지, 항아리

143. pour [pɔːr] – to cause to flow in a stream 따르다, 쏟다

144. powder [páudər] – very small and fine pieces of something, such as flour or gunpowder 가루, 분말

145. pray [prei] – to talk with a god 기도하다

146. pretend [priténd] – to make believe with the intent to deceive ~인 체하다

147. priest [priːst] – a religious leader who performs religious duties 성직자

148. professor [prəfésər] – a high ranking instructor at a university or college 교수

149. proof [pruːf] – something that proves 증거

150. prove [pruːv] – to give proof for; to give evidence for; to show something to be true 증명하다

151. publish [pʌ́bliʃ] – to print a book 출판하다

152. punch [pʌntʃ] – to hit using a closed fist 주먹으로 치다

153. receive [risíːv] – to get or be given something 받다

154. recipe [résəpìː] - the instructions for making a food or drink 영수증

155. record [rékərd] - an official written document that gives proof of something or tells about past events 기록

156. reef [riːf] - an underwater rock or coral near the water's surface 암초

157. refuse [rifjúːz] - to say that you will not accept; be unwilling to do 거절하다

158. register [rédʒəstər] - a record of names or events 기록부

159. replace [ripléis] - to be used instead of something 대신하다

160. reply [riplái] - to respond to a question, statement, or a written message 대답하다

161. respect [rispékt] - to hold in high regards 존경하다

162. rise [raiz] - to move upward; to move to a higher position 일어서다

163. riverbank [rívərbæ̀ŋk] - the land on the sides of a river 둑

164. roll [roul] - to move by turning over and over on a surface 구르다

165. rooster [rúːstər] - an adult male chicken 수탉

166. root [ruːt] - the part of a plant that is underground, absorbs water and minerals, and anchors the plant 뿌리

167. rope [roup] - a strong line, similar to a thick string 줄, 끈

168. row [rou] - the arrangement of objects of people in a straight line 열

169. rude [ruːd] - impolite; acting without care for others 무례한

170. rumor [rúːmər] - a story repeated by many people which may be true or false 소문

171. rush [rʌʃ] - to move quickly; to do something quickly 돌진하다

Key Word 240

172. sail [seil] – to travel by ship 항해하다

173. scale [skeil] – an object used to weigh things 저울

174. scar [skɑːr] – a mark left on the skin after injury 상처

175. scarecrow [skɛ́ərkròu] – a large doll used to scare away birds 허수아비

176. scent [sent] – a pleasant smell that is produced by something 향기

177. score [skɔːr] – the number of points, goals, runs, etc., that each player or team has in a game or contest 득점, 성적

178. scream [skriːm] – to make a loud, high-pitched sound, usually because of extreme fear or excitement 소리치다

179. screech [skriːtʃ] – make a high-pitched noise like a scream 날카로운 소리

180. seem [siːm] – to give a certain impression ~으로 보이다

181. self-portrait [sélfpɔ́ːrtrit] – a picture one makes of oneself 자화상

182. separate [sépərèit] – to force or take apart; to cause to stopo being together or connected 분리하다

183. servant [sə́ːrvənt] – a person whose job is to serve another person, especially in their home 하인

184. serve [səːrv] – to give as a meal 봉사하다

185. sew [sou] – to use a needle and thread to join cloth together 꿰매다

186. shave [ʃeiv] – to remove of the hairs from something using a blade 면도하다

187. shine [ʃain] – to release light; to send out light 비추다, 빛나다

188. shy [ʃai] – timid; hesitant to talk to others; having little self-confidence 소심한, 부끄러워하는

189. similar [símələr] – like; having a resemblance to 비슷한

190. **since** [sins] – indicates the beginning of an activity or state which continues to the present ~이래로

191. **sink** [siŋk] – to go under water 가라앉다

192. **sketch** [sketch] – to make quick and simple drawings 스케치하다

193. **skill** [skil] – ability to do something, especially when experienced 솜씨

194. **skillful** [skílfəl] – full of skill; having a lot of skill 능숙한

195. **slice** [slais] – a thin piece of something that was made by cutting it from a larger piece 얇은 조각

196. **sob** [sɑb] – to cry very hard 흐느껴 울다

197. **soda** [sóudə] – a kind of cold drink with carbonation 탄산수

198. **something** [sʌ́mθiŋ] – a thing of some kind 무언가

199. **spell** [spel] – to say or write the letters of Word in the correct order 철자를 말하다

200. **spend** [spend] – to pass time in a certain way; to use money 소비하다

201. **spill** [spil] – to cause to pour out 엎지르다

202. **spirit** [spírit] – a supernatural being 정신

203. **spot** [spɑt] – a small area of a surface that is different from other areas 점, 얼룩

204. **spread** [spred] – to move out widely; to become widely known 펴다

205. **stab** [stæb] – to put a knife or other sharp object into someone or something (칼로) 찌르다

206. **starve** [stɑːrv] – to suffer or die from lack of food 굶주리다, 굶어죽다

Key Word 240

207. stick [stik] – a long, thin piece of wood 막대기

208. sting [stiŋ] – to put a stinger into another animal (침 등으로) 찌르다

209. stove [stouv] – an item that uses heat to cook food 난로

210. strike [straik] – to hit in a forceful way 치다

211. string [striŋ] – a material like thick thread or a thin rope 끈, 줄

212. subtract [səbtrǽkt] – to decrease by subtraction 빼다

213. express [iksprés] – to talk or write about 표현하다

214. survive [sərváiv] – to live through a difficult situation 살아남다

215. swallow [swɑ́lou] – to take something into your stomach 삼키다

216. sword [sɔːrd] – a long blade attached to a handle 칼

217. tadpole [tǽdpòul] – a baby frog before it has legs that lives in the water 올챙이

218. tailor [téilər] – a person who sews and makes clothes 재단사

219. tap [tæp] – to hit softly 가볍게 두드리다

220. target [tɑ́ːrgit] – something that you are trying to do or achieve; a place, thing, or person at which an attack is aimed 목표, 표적

221. tear [tɛər] – a drop of water from the eyes when crying; to separate by pulling apart 눈물, 찢다

222. telescope [téləskòup] – an object that allows a person to see very far 망원경

223. threaten [θrétn] – to make a threat; to warn someone of danger if a condition is not met 위협하다

224. thrust [θrʌst] – to believe that someone or something is reliable, good, honest, etc. 믿다

225. **tie** [tai] – a strip of cloth that is tied around the neck and usually worn with suits; to make a knot 넥타이, 묶다

226. **till** [til] – up to the time of ~까지

227. **tombstone** [túːmstòun] – a stone placed to mark a grave, usually with writing on it 묘비

228. **traitor** [tréitər] – a person who betrays 배반자, 배신자

229. **tremble** [trémbəl] – to shake slightly because you are afraid, nervous, excited, etc. 떨다

230. **trick** [trik] – a cunning action; a deceitful action 속임수

231. **trouble** [trʌ́bəl] – problems or difficulties 곤란, 문제

232. **trust** [trʌst] – the act of believing; having confidence in 신뢰

233. **upset** [ʌpsét] – disturbed; unhappy and worried 당황한, 걱정한

234. **vacation** [veikéiʃən] – a period of time that a person spends away from school, or business to relax or travel 휴가, 방학

235. **wander** [wɑ́ndər] – to walk around without a destination 헤매다, 거닐다

236. **weight** [weit] – the amount something weighs 무게

237. **width** [widθ] – the measurement from one side to the other that is not the longest length 너비

238. **winner** [wínər] – a person who wins 우승자

239. **wire** [waiər] – a long, metal string 철사

240. **wisdom** [wízdəm] – ability to use intelligence with common sense; knowledge gained through experience 지혜

Word List 960 (단어 – 단어번호)

- A -

able - 59
abroad - 884
absent - 583
achieve - 892
across - 567
act - 277
actor - 959
address - 372
adventure - 946
afraid - 5
after - 46
afternoon - 43
again - 282
age - 807
ago - 422
agree - 937
air - 273
airplane - 355
airport - 537
album - 803
all1 - 91
allow - 842
almost - 903
alone - 485
also - 747
always - 184
among - 951
and - 502
angel - 861
angry - 590
animal - 395
another - 506
answer - 151
ant - 449
any - 546
apartment - 663
appear - 656
apple - 241
area - 923
arm - 38
around - 314
arrive - 295
arrow - 949
art - 718
artist - 942
as - 403
ask - 318
attack - 234
aunt - 215
autumn - 44
away - 36
ax - 641

- B -

baby - 231
back - 55
backward - 64
bad - 158
bag - 35
baker - 627
ball - 349
balloon - 102
bank - 577
baseball - 919
basket - 188
bat - 418
bath - 775
beach - 725
bean - 266
bear - 171
beat - 954
beautiful - 228
because - 593
become - 49
bed - 586
bedroom - 628
bee - 187
beef - 10
before - 406
begin - 539
behind - 489
believe - 824
bell - 413
belong - 845
below - 814
belt - 293
bench - 670
beside - 740
best - 600
between - 492
bicycle - 50
big - 216
bird - 205
birthday - 733
black - 236
blanket - 504
blow - 612
blue - 253
board - 710
boat2 - 99
body - 16

boil - 794
bone - 746
book - 41
boot - 399
boring - 862
borrow - 579
both - 142
bottle - 136
bowl - 310
box - 193
boy - 217
brave - 763
bread - 145
break - 909
breakfast - 526
brick - 914
bridge - 767
bright - 944
bring - 285
brother - 468
brown - 270
brush - 129
build - 765
bull - 354
bus - 732
busy - 598
but - 267
butter - 702
button - 80
buy - 484
by - 429

- C -

cage - 943

cake - 805
calendar - 729
call - 57
camera - 796
can - 37
candle - 431
candy - 544
cap - 172
capital - 79
captain - 768
car - 498
card - 762
care - 781
careful - 674
carrot - 784
carry - 88
cat - 15
catch - 463
center - 150
chair - 225
chalk - 173
challenge - 936
chance - 929
change - 578
cheap - 419
check - 442
cheese - 715
chef - 935
chess - 131
chest - 240
chicken - 31
child - 572
chin - 437
choose - 665

chopsticks - 85
church - 100
city - 177
class - 430
classmate - 772
clean - 309
clever - 706
climb - 325
clock - 244
close - 458
clothes - 242
cloud - 423
club - 681
coat - 730
coffee - 811
coin - 661
cold - 2
collect - 848
color - 198
comb - 369
come - 554
company - 948
computer - 592
contest - 818
cook - 39
cookie - 78
cool - 550
copy - 646
corner - 474
correct - 825
cotton - 804
count - 159
country - 330
cousin - 106

Word List 960

cover - 381
cow - 81
crayon - 698
crazy - 896
cry - 196
cucumber - 956
culture - 853
cup - 257
curtain - 933
cut - 450
cute - 508

- D -

dance - 401
danger - 819
dangerous - 669
dark - 505
date - 581
daughter - 232
day - 286
dead - 685
decide - 735
deep - 404
deer - 645
delicious - 866
dentist - 252
desk - 26
diary - 6
dictionary - 827
die - 130
difference - 874
different - 859
difficult - 885
dig - 629
dining room - 478
dinner - 368
dirty - 327
discover - 894
dish - 294
distance - 922
divide - 939
do - 562
doctor - 341
dog - 220
doll - 118
dollar - 22
dolphin - 552
donkey - 792
door - 457
down - 490
draw - 466
dream - 750
dress - 791
drink - 556
drive - 658
drop - 809
drum - 617
dry - 396
duck - 148
during - 638

- E -

each - 167
ear - 378
early - 324
earth - 597
east - 137
easy - 14
eat - 387
education - 886
egg - 305
either - 60
elephant - 54
empty - 659
end - 94
enemy - 912
energy - 867
enjoy - 108
enough - 955
enter - 722
equal - 708
evening - 326
every - 283
exam - 882
example - 618
excellent - 849
excited - 952
excuse - 69
exercise - 679
expensive - 383
experiment - 945
explain - 673
eye - 65

- F -

face - 170
fact - 684
fake - 666
fall - 560
family - 436
famous - 664
far - 398

farm - 317
farmer - 834
fashion - 851
fast - 141
fat - 358
father - 250
favor - 910
favorite - 847
feather - 709
feed - 704
feel - 890
fence - 697
fever - 1
few - 759
field - 275
fight - 752
fill - 829
film - 199
finally - 893
find - 185
fine - 33
finger - 339
finish - 482
fire - 693
fish - 34
flag - 464
floor - 433
flower - 214
fly - 233
fold - 771
follow - 446
food - 558
fool - 738
foolish - 680

foot - 467
footprint - 689
foreign - 858
forget - 758
forgive - 683
forward - 930
found - 826
fox - 246
free - 146
freedom - 823
fresh - 644
friend - 27
friendship - 789
frog - 417
front - 166
fruit - 284
fry - 904
full - 70
fun - 243
funny - 780

- G -

gallery - 916
garden - 496
gas - 614
gate - 135
gather - 764
gentle - 773
get - 212
ghost - 662
giant - 745
gift - 941
girl - 113
give - 477

glad - 322
glass - 62
go - 82
goat - 432
god - 812
goddess - 675
gold - 84
golden - 237
good - 511
grandfather - 321
grandmother - 343
grape - 720
grass - 636
grasshopper - 802
gray - 487
great - 278
greedy - 595
green - 221
greet6 - 77
ground - 699
grow - 410
guess - 860
guest - 682

- H -

hair - 384
hairpin - 601
half - 291
hall - 769
hand - 289
handsome - 691
happen - 686
happy - 229
hard - 536

Word List 960

harp - 245
hate - 400
have - 96
head - 491
health - 865
hear - 839
heart - 640
heaven - 801
heavy - 3
helicopter - 412
help - 24
hen - 727
here - 459
hide - 654
high - 344
hill - 833
hit - 643
hobby - 370
hold - 564
hole - 648
home - 366
honest - 881
hope - 138
horse - 338
hospital - 553
hot - 116
hotel - 140
hour - 206
house - 342
how - 571
human - 737
hundred - 531
hungry - 77
hunt - 841

hunter - 928
hurt - 603

- I -

ice - 761
idea - 434
if - 649
ill - 175
important - 934
in - 218
information - 878
ink - 723
insect - 795
inside - 124
instead - 888
interesting - 741
into - 52
introduce - 837
invention - 835
invitation - 495
invite - 668
island - 776

- J, K -

jacket - 389
jam - 288
jeans - 111
job - 960
join - 869
jump - 447
jungle - 766
just - 416
keep - 573
kid - 624

kill - 195
kind - 269
king - 132
kingdom - 690
kitchen - 488
kite - 635
knee - 525
knife - 162
knight - 607
knock - 251
know - 181

- L -

ladder - 756
lady - 361
lake - 631
lamb - 754
lamp - 147
land - 523
large - 121
last - 908
late - 190
laugh - 194
law - 857
lay - 497
leader - 787
leaf - 734
learn - 402
leave - 634
left - 287
leg - 110
lend - 953
lesson - 435
let - 311

letter - 393
library - 808
lie - 652
life - 47
light - 262
like - 335
line - 671
lion - 373
listen - 461
little - 650
live - 534
living room - 201
lock - 921
long - 424
look - 315
lose - 907
lot - 854
loud - 104
love - 303
low - 331
luck - 117
lunch - 207

- M -

machine - 905
mad - 276
magic - 451
mail - 407
mailman - 713
main - 880
make - 512
man - 247
many - 235
map - 76

market - 176
marry - 87
math - 623
matter - 816
may - 174
maybe - 149
meal - 120
mean - 915
meat - 345
medal - 810
medicine - 798
meet - 500
melt - 925
milk - 541
million - 549
mind - 705
minus - 783
minutev - 227
mirror - 426
miss - 48
mistake - 876
mix - 918
money - 155
monkey - 304
monster - 469
month - 391
moon - 460
morning - 307
mother - 456
mountain - 596
mouse - 91
mouth - 66
move - 509
movie - 385

much - 411
museum - 846
music - 409
musician - 653
must - 527

- N -

name - 352
nature - 901
near - 751
neck - 386
need - 532
neighbor - 877
nephew - 392
never - 347
new - 165
news - 178
next - 778
nice - 83
niece - 332
night - 503
noise - 637
noon - 510
north - 415
nose - 448
note - 728
now - 582
number - 374
nurse - 364

- O -

o'clock - 800
object - 748
off - 414

Word List 960

office - 323
often - 312
oil - 18
old - 67
once - 517
only - 726
open - 475
or - 444
order - 632
origin - 938
other - 223
out - 507
outside - 25
over - 125

- P -

page - 63
paint - 379
painter - 357
painting - 947
pair - 891
palace - 760
pants - 297
paper - 298
parents - 348
park - 20
pass - 470
past - 569
patient - 676
pay - 95
peace - 604
pear - 421
pearl - 518
pebble - 633

pencil - 445
people - 239
pepper - 157
perfect - 872
person - 565
photo - 613
piano - 200
pick - 408
picnic - 875
picture - 122
piece - 620
pig - 420
pineapple - 701
pipe - 642
place - 736
plan - 744
plant - 611
play - 256
please - 68
plus - 889
pocket - 265
point - 486
police - 51
pool - 619
poor - 538
popular - 852
pork - 28
possible - 906
post - 109
potato - 563
power - 855
practice - 932
present - 667
pretty - 319

prince - 714
princess - 743
print - 774
problem - 568
promise - 863
pull - 29
punish - 753
puppy - 73
purple - 483
push - 209
put - 53
pyramid - 755

- Q, R -

quarrel - 688
queen - 164
question - 473
quick - 382
quiet - 522
quite - 856
rabbit - 528
race - 844
rain - 443
raise - 898
reach - 785
read - 360
ready - 75
real - 695
rectangle - 454
red - 115
refrigerator - 376
remember - 821
repeat - 731
rescue - 899

rest - 32
restaurant - 639
return - 900
rice - 126
rich - 380
ride - 545
right - 427
ring - 30
river - 259
road - 363
rock - 40
rocket - 672
roof - 895
room - 208
rose - 719
round - 112
rule - 927
run - 61

- S -

sad - 261
safe - 499
salt - 622
same - 230
sand - 9
sandwich - 337
save - 820
say - 439
scared - 630
school - 203
science - 871
scorpion - 742
sea - 428
season - 559

seat - 290
see - 156
select - 711
sell - 71
seller - 452
send - 103
service - 917
set - 260
several - 957
shadow - 931
shape - 703
sharp - 887
sheep - 717
ship - 97
shocked - 924
shoe - 281
shop - 98
short - 346
shoulder - 479
shout - 566
show - 472
sick - 438
side - 548
silver - 712
simple - 873
sing - 519
sister - 362
sit - 465
size - 133
skin - 840
skirt - 425
sky - 72
sleep - 279
slow - 316

small - 222
smart - 180
smell - 74
smile - 329
snake - 271
snow - 127
so - 255
soap - 313
soccer - 367
socks - 365
soft - 21
soldier - 696
some - 192
son - 371
song - 515
soon - 822
sorrow - 920
sorry - 139
sound - 757
sour - 168
south - 101
space - 616
speak - 576
special - 870
speech - 926
speed - 694
spider - 786
spoon - 397
spring - 86
square - 45
stair - 471
stamp - 301
stand - 455
star - 306

Word List 960

start - 300
station - 587
stay - 529
steal - 621
steam - 843
step - 739
still - 958
stomach - 707
stone - 700
stop - 585
store - 353
storm - 615
story - 513
strange - 655
straw - 897
street - 481
strong - 264
student - 197
study - 359
stupid - 375
subway - 153
succeed - 879
sugar - 263
summer - 58
sun - 154
sunflower - 462
sunny - 657
supermarket - 660
supper - 292
sure - 128
surprised - 940
sweet - 272
swim - 480
swing - 797

switch - 589

- T -
table - 453
tail - 788
take - 105
talk - 302
tall - 93
taste - 817
taxi - 836
tea - 56
teach - 254
team - 114
telephone - 575
television - 160
tell - 551
temple - 813
tennis - 524
test - 626
than - 258
thank - 134
that - 211
theater - 850
then - 515
there - 17
thick - 501
thief - 806
thin - 334
thing - 19
think - 274
thirsty - 90
this - 340
thousand - 533
through - 107

throw - 782
thumb - 143
ticket - 602
tiger - 163
time - 189
tired - 186
today - 224
toe - 610
together - 520
toilet - 182
tomato - 594
tomorrow - 377
tonight - 356
too - 169
tooth - 213
top - 647
total - 724
touch - 868
toward - 651
towel - 11
tower - 777
town - 493
toy - 123
train - 336
travel - 770
treasure - 793
tree - 219
triangle - 514
truck - 913
true - 570
try - 308
tulip - 606
turn - 12
twice - 832

twins - 625

- U, V -
ugly - 183
uncle - 328
understand - 588
unhappy - 864
university - 716
until - 530
up - 280
use - 521
usual - 902
vegetable - 535
very - 89
victory - 831
view - 960
village - 827
visit - 440
voice - 815

- W -
wait - 13
wake - 119
walk - 99
wall - 692
want - 547
war - 609
warm - 540
wash - 296
waste - 883
watch - 23
water - 350
wave - 911
way - 390
weak - 42
wear - 248
week - 92
welcome - 161
well - 494
west - 204
wet - 779
what - 561
when - 557
where - 543
which - 580
white - 210
who - 584
whose - 830
why - 574
wide - 394
wife - 749
wild - 799
will - 542
win - 7
wind - 268
window - 320
wing - 333
winter - 599
wise - 721
wish - 678
without - 687
wolf - 838
woman - 238
wood - 790
woods - 608
word - 555
work - 226
worker - 351
world - 405
worry - 591
write - 8
wrong - 476

- X, Y, Z -
yard - 605
yawn - 179
year - 441
yellow - 388
yesterday - 4
young - 249
zebra - 144
zero - 202
zoo - 152

Weekly Test 1 (Unit 1~5)

* 영어는 우리말로, 우리말은 영어로 써 보세요.

1. heavy _____   2. body _____

3. fish _____   4. weak _____

5. summer _____   6. 모래 _____

7. 쉬운 _____   8. 끌다, 당기다 _____

9. 정사각형 _____   10. 자전거 _____

* 우리말과 같은 뜻이 되도록 빈칸을 채워보세요.

11. I had a _____ yesterday. 나는 어제 열이 났었다.

12. Please _____ for a moment. 잠시만 기다려 주세요.

13. It will be _____ tomorrow. 내일은 날씨가 맑을 것이다.

14. Ann is sitting on the _____. Ann은 바위 위에 앉아 있다.

15. Ice will _____ water. 얼음은 물이 될 것이다.

* 단어의 뜻에 맞게 빈칸에 알맞은 단어를 쓰세요.

16. _____ : feeling very smooth to the touch

17. _____ : a person who cooks; to prepare food by heating it

Test 2 정답 | 1. 입 2. 강아지 3. 키가 큰 4. 남쪽 5. 둥근 6. glass 7. hungry 8. chosticks 9. church 10. red 11. run 12. goid 13. week 14. balloon 15. jeans 16. sell 17. pay

Weekly Test 2 (Unit 6~10)

* 영어는 우리말로, 우리말은 영어로 써 보세요.

1. mouth _____   2. puppy _____
3. tall _____   4. south _____
5. round _____   6. 유리, 컵 _____
7. 배고픈 _____   8. 젓가락 _____
9. 교회 _____   10. 빨간, 적색의 _____

* 우리말과 같은 뜻이 되도록 빈칸을 채워보세요.

11. I can _____ fast. 나는 빨리 달릴 수 있다.

12. I have a _____ ring. 나는 금반지를 가지고 있다.

13. There are seven days in a _____. 일주일은 7일이다.

14. My _____ is flying away! 내 풍선이 날아간다.

15. These _____ are too tight. 이 청바지는 꽉 낀다.

* 단어의 뜻에 맞게 빈칸에 알맞은 단어를 쓰세요.

16. _____ : to exchange something for money

17. _____ : to give money for something you buy or for a service

Test 1 정답 | 1. 무거운 2. 몸 3. 물고기 4. 약한 5. 여름 6. sand 7. easy 8. pull 9. square 10. bicycle(bike) 11. fever 12. wait 13. fine 14. rock 15. become 16. soft 17. cook

Weekly Test 3 (Unit 11~15)

* 영어는 우리말로, 우리말은 영어로 써 보세요.

1. picture _____   2. thumb _____
3. bread _____   4. count _____
5. smart _____   6. 장난감 _____
7. 감사하다 _____   8. 태양 _____
9. 여왕 _____   10. 곰 _____

* 우리말과 같은 뜻이 되도록 빈칸을 채워보세요.

11. The lion is a _____ of animals. 사자는 동물 중의 왕이다.

12. Rabbits are so _____. 토끼는 매우 빠르다.

13. The _____ is correct. 그 대답이 맞다.

14. I bought a _____ jacket. 나는 새 재킷을 샀다.

15. Seoul is a big _____. 서울은 큰 도시이다.

* 단어의 뜻에 맞게 빈칸에 알맞은 단어를 쓰세요.

16. _____ : a door which is set up to block the entrance of something

17. _____ : a place where animals are kept for people to see

Test 4 정답 | 1. 알다 2. 웃다 3. 방 4. 아름다운 5. 같은 6. basket 7. school 8. push 9. green 10. daughter 11. late 12. zero 13. tooth 14. today 15. happy 16. student 17. flower

Weekly Test 4 (Unit 16~20)

* 영어는 우리말로, 우리말은 영어로 써 보세요.

1. know _____
2. laugh _____
3. room _____
4. beautiful _____
5. same _____
6. 바구니 _____
7. 학교 _____
8. 밀다 _____
9. 녹색의 _____
10. 딸 _____

* 우리말과 같은 뜻이 되도록 빈칸을 채워보세요.

11. I was _____ for school. 나는 학교에 늦었다.

12. The score is five to _____. 점수는 5 대 0이다.

13. The baby has one _____. 아기는 이가 한 개 있다.

14. What day is it _____? 오늘은 무슨 요일이니?

15. I am _____ with you. 나는 너와 함께 있어서 행복하다.

* 단어의 뜻에 맞게 빈칸에 알맞은 단어를 쓰세요.

16. _____ : someone who studies, especially at a school

17. _____ : a plant that has petals and leaves

Test 3 정답 | 1. 그림, 사진 2. 엄지손가락 3. 빵 4. 세다 5. 영리한 6. toy 7. thank 8. sun 9. queen 10. bear 11. king 12. fast 13. answer 14. new 15. city 16. gate 17. zoo

Weekly Test 5 (Unit 21~25)

* 영어는 우리말로, 우리말은 영어로 써 보세요.

1. young _____
2. light _____
3. bean _____
4. bring _____
5. paper _____
6. 시계 _____
7. 슬픈 _____
8. 생각하다 _____
9. 신발, 구두 _____
10. 시작하다 _____

* 우리말과 같은 뜻이 되도록 빈칸을 채워보세요.

11. Playing is _____. 노는 것이 재미있다.

12. It is big and _____. 그것은 크고 튼튼하다.

13. My _____ is full. 나의 주머니가 가득하다.

14. He _____ like a child. 그는 어린이처럼 행동한다.

15. Place the fruit on this _____. 이 접시에 그 과일을 놓아라.

* 단어의 뜻에 맞게 빈칸에 알맞은 단어를 쓰세요.

16. _____ : to have on one's body, as in clothing or jewelry

17. _____ : something made to sit on

Test 6 정답 | 1. 종종, 자주 2. 주위에 3. 얇은 4. 손가락 5. 물 6. try 7. glad 8. wing 9. meat 10. tonight 11. love 12. ask 13. dirty 14. high 15. read 16. star 17. train

Weekly Test 6 (Unit 26~30)

* 영어는 우리말로, 우리말은 영어로 써 보세요.

1. often _____   2. around _____

3. thin _____   4. finger _____

5. water _____   6. 노력하다 _____

7. 기쁜 _____   8. 날개 _____

9. 고기 _____   10. 오늘밤에 _____

* 우리말과 같은 뜻이 되도록 빈칸을 채워보세요.

11. I _____ mom and dad. 나는 엄마와 아빠를 사랑한다.

12. May I _____ a question? 질문해도 될까요?

13. We clean up the _____ room. 우리는 더러운 방을 청소한다.

14. The wall is very _____. 그 벽은 매우 높다.

15. I _____ three books yesterday. 나는 어제 책 3권을 읽었다.

* 단어의 뜻에 맞게 빈칸에 알맞은 단어를 쓰세요.

16. _____ : a ball of gas in the sky that shines

17. _____ : a group of connected carriages that move on a railroad

---

Test 5 정답 | 1. 젊은, 어린 2. 전등 3. 콩 4. 가져오다 5. 종이 6. clock 7. sad 8. think 9. shoe 10. start 11. fun 12. strong 13. pocket 14. acts 15. dish 16. wear 17. seat

Weekly Test 7 (Unit 31~35)

* 영어는 우리말로, 우리말은 영어로 써 보세요.

1. lady _____   2. expensive _____

3. movie _____   4. world _____

5. music _____   6. 빗, 빗질하다 _____

7. 부유한 _____   8. 동물 _____

9. 배우다 _____   10. 개구리 _____

* 우리말과 같은 뜻이 되도록 빈칸을 채워보세요.

11. That _____ is very wide. 저 길은 매우 넓다.

12. He is leaving _____. 그는 내일 떠날 예정이다.

13. I like that black _____. 나는 저 검정색 재킷이 맘에 든다.

14. The hole is very _____. 그 구멍은 매우 깊다.

15. The _____ is ringing. 그 종이 울리고 있다.

* 단어의 뜻에 맞게 빈칸에 알맞은 단어를 쓰세요.

16. _____ : an activity that you regularly do for pleasure

17. _____ : to astrongly dislike someone or something

Test 8 정답 | 1. 양초 2. 바다, 층 3. 따르다 4. 달 5. 보여주다 6. cloud 7. family 8. magic 9. flag 10. open 11. sea 12. check 13. jumps 14. listens 15. Pass 16. mirror 17. question

Weekly Test 8 (Unit 36~40)

* 영어는 우리말로, 우리말은 영어로 써 보세요.

1. candle _____   2. floor _____

3. follow _____   4. moon _____

5. show _____   6. 구름 _____

7. 가족 _____   8. 마술, 마력 _____

9. 깃발 _____   10. 열다 _____

* 우리말과 같은 뜻이 되도록 빈칸을 채워보세요.

11. I can swim in the _____. 나는 바다에서 수영할 수 있다.

12. Go and _____ your accounts. 가서 너의 계산서를 점검해라.

13. She _____ forward three times. 그녀는 앞으로 3번 뛴다.

14. My sister _____ to rock music. 나의 누나는 락 음악을 듣는다.

15. _____ me some salt, please. 나에게 소금을 좀 주세요.

* 단어의 뜻에 맞게 빈칸에 알맞은 단어를 쓰세요.

16. _____ : a smooth or polished surface that reflects images

17. _____ : something that you ask someone

Test 7 정답 | 1. 숙녀 2. 비싼 3. 영화 4. 세계 5. 음악 6. comb 7. rich 8. animal 9. learn 10. frog 11. road 12. tomorrow 13. jacket 14. deep 15. bell 16. hobby 17. hate

Weekly Test 9 (Unit 41~45)

* 영어는 우리말로, 우리말은 영어로 써 보세요.

1. finish _____
2. invitation _____
3. cute _____
4. pearl _____
5. need _____
6. 머리 _____
7. 시내, 읍 _____
8. 만들다 _____
9. 아침식사 _____
10. 따뜻한 _____

* 우리말과 같은 뜻이 되도록 빈칸을 채워보세요.

11. I will be _____ at home tomorrow. 나는 내일 집에 혼자 있을 것이다.

12. Her _____ is clean. 그녀의 담요는 깨끗하다.

13. It is a _____ about good men. 그것은 좋은 사람들에 대한 이야기이다.

14. Be _____ in the museum. 박물관에서는 조용히 하세요.

15. I have to work _____ five. 나는 5시까지 일해야 한다.

* 단어의 뜻에 맞게 빈칸에 알맞은 단어를 쓰세요.

16. _____ : a place where people grow flowers or plants

17. _____ : to make music with one's voice

Test 10 정답 | 1. 돌고래 2. 감자 3. 사람 4. 빌리다 5. 지구 6. milk 7. season 8. real 9. change 10. winter 11. ride 12. came 13. across 14. bed 15. angry 16. food 17. tomato

Weekly Test 10 (Unit 46~50)

* 영어는 우리말로, 우리말은 영어로 써 보세요.

1. dolphin _____
2. potato _____
3. person _____
4. borrow _____
5. earth _____
6. 우유 _____
7. 계절 _____
8. 진실의, 사실의 _____
9. 바꾸다 _____
10. 겨울 _____

* 우리말과 같은 뜻이 되도록 빈칸을 채워보세요.

11. I like to _____ a bike. 나는 자전거 타는 것을 좋아한다.

12. He _____ to my house. 그는 나의 집에 왔다.

13. The girl is _____ the street. 그 소녀는 길 건너편에 있다.

14. My _____ is very comfortable. 나의 침대는 매우 편하다.

15. He is _____ with me. 그는 나에게 화가 나 있다.

* 단어의 뜻에 맞게 빈칸에 알맞은 단어를 쓰세요.

16. _____ : something which is eaten and is necessary for life

17. _____ : a red fruit that is used to make ketchup

Test 9 정답 | 1. 끝내다 2. 초대 3. 귀여운 4. 진주 5. 필요하다 6. head 7. town 8. make 9. breakfast 10. warm 11. alone 12. blanket 13. story 14. quiet 15. until 16. garden 17. sing

Weekly Test 11 (Unit 51~55)

* 영어는 우리말로, 우리말은 영어로 써 보세요.

1. knight _____
2. example _____
3. kite _____
4. restaurant _____
5. musician _____
6. 평화 _____
7. 훔치다 _____
8. 시험, 검사 _____
9. 사슴 _____
10. 나타나다 _____

* 우리말과 같은 뜻이 되도록 빈칸을 채워보세요.

11. I _____ my hands yesterday. 나는 어제 내 손을 다쳤다.

12. She cut the cake in eight _____. 그녀는 케이크를 8조각으로 잘랐다.

13. We have three _____. 우리는 침실이 3개 있다.

14. I like _____ vegetables. 나는 신선한 야채를 좋아한다.

15. My mom can _____ the car well. 나의 엄마는 차를 잘 운전하신다.

* 단어의 뜻에 맞게 빈칸에 알맞은 단어를 쓰세요.

16. _____ : an area of land that is next to a building

17. _____ : without anything inside

Test 12 정답 | 1. 유명한 2. 설명하다 3. 발생하다 4. 땅, 지역 5. 선택하다 6. apartment 7. guest 8. footpoint 9. feed 10. university 11. rocket 12. patient 13. wall 14. shape 15. prince 16. dangerous 17. butter

Weekly Test 12 (Unit 56~60)

* 영어는 우리말로, 우리말은 영어로 써 보세요.

1. famous _____
2. explain _____
3. happen _____
4. ground _____
5. select _____
6. 아파트 _____
7. 손님 _____
8. 발자국 _____
9. 먹이를 주다 _____
10. 대학 _____

* 우리말과 같은 뜻이 되도록 빈칸을 채워보세요.

11. They are carrying the _____. 그들은 로켓을 운반하고 있다.

12. The _____ will get well soon. 그 환자는 금방 나을 것이다.

13. I am going to paint the _____ white. 나는 벽을 흰색으로 칠할 것이다.

14. The pool is in the _____ of a heart. 그 수영장은 하트 모양이다.

15. The _____ is brave and clever. 그 왕자는 용감하고 똑똑하다.

* 단어의 뜻에 맞게 빈칸에 알맞은 단어를 쓰세요.

16. _____ : involving danger or risk; not safe

17. _____ : a solid yellowish food that is made from the cream of milk

Test 11 정답 | 1. 기사 2. 예, 보기 3. 연 4. 식당 5. 음악가 6. peace 7. steal 8. test 9. deer 10. appear 11. hurt 12. pieces 13. bedrooms 14. fresh 15. drive 16. yard 17. empty

Weekly Test 13 (Unit 61~65)

* 영어는 우리말로, 우리말은 영어로 써 보세요.

1. calendar _____
2. decide _____
3. punish _____
4. sound _____
5. tower _____
6. 현명한 _____
7. 걸음, 단계 _____
8. 물건, 물체 _____
9. 다리 _____
10. 섬 _____

* 우리말과 같은 뜻이 되도록 빈칸을 채워보세요.

11. Can you _____ your question? 질문을 다시 말씀해주시겠습니까?
12. The knight danced with the _____. 그 기사는 공주와 춤을 추었다.
13. This fish has a lot of _____ in it. 이 생선은 뼈가 많다.
14. Many people _____ in the square. 많은 사람들이 광장에 모였다.
15. The clothes are still _____. 그 옷은 아직도 젖어 있다.

* 단어의 뜻에 맞게 빈칸에 알맞은 단어를 쓰세요.

16. _____ : the sandy land along a sea or ocean
17. _____ : a student in the same class as another

Test 14 정답 | 1. 당근 2. 천국 3. 목소리 4. 믿다 5. 승리 6. wood 7. swing 8. thief 9. remember 10. skin 11. minus 12. wild 13. library 14. correct 15. hill 16. friendship 17. hear

Weekly Test 14 (Unit 66~70)

* 영어는 우리말로, 우리말은 영어로 써 보세요.

1. carrot _____
2. heaven _____
3. voice _____
4. believe _____
5. victory _____
6. 나무, 목재 _____
7. 그네 _____
8. 도둑 _____
9. 기억하다 _____
10. 피부 _____

* 우리말과 같은 뜻이 되도록 빈칸을 채워보세요.

11. Seven _____ four is three. 7 빼기 4는 3이다.

12. I looked at a _____ rabbit. 나는 야생 토끼를 보았다.

13. I always go to the _____. 나는 매일 도서관에 간다.

14. Your answers are _____. 너의 정답들이 정확하다.

15. We are running to the _____. 우리는 언덕으로 뛰어가고 있다.

* 단어의 뜻에 맞게 빈칸에 알맞은 단어를 쓰세요.

16. _____ : the state of being friends

17. _____ : to notice something through your ears

Test 13 정답 | 1. 달력 2. 결정하다 3. 별주다 4. 소리 5. 탑, 타워 6. wise 7. step 8. object 9. bridge 10. island 11. repeat 12. princess 13. bones 14. gathered 15. wet 16. beach 17. classmate

Weekly Test 15 (Unit 71~75)

* 영어는 우리말로, 우리말은 영어로 써 보세요.

1. excellent _____
2. boring _____
3. touch _____
4. neighbor _____
5. finally _____
6. 사냥하다 _____
7. 추측하다 _____
8. 차이 _____
9. 날카로운 _____
10. 지붕 _____

* 우리말과 같은 뜻이 되도록 빈칸을 채워보세요.

11. I _____ stamps and postcards. 나는 우표와 엽서를 모았다.

12. I traveled to a lot of _____ countries.
    나는 외국의 많은 나라를 여행했다.

13. This machine is very _____ to use.
    이 기계는 사용하는 게 매우 간단하다.

14. She is a kind and _____ girl. 그녀는 친절하고 정직한 소녀이다.

15. The man is drinking with a _____.
    그 남자는 빨대로 이용해 마시고 있다.

* 단어의 뜻에 맞게 빈칸에 알맞은 단어를 쓰세요.

16. _____ : the ability or right to control people or things

17. _____ : a trip that includes a meal eaten outdoors

Test 16 정답 | 1. 자연 2. 벽돌 3. 중요한 4. 모험 5. 화살 6. last 7. mean 8. curtain 9. orgin 10. actor 11. fry 12. area 13. melt 14. company 15. still 16. distance 17. gift

Weekly Test 16 (Unit 76~80)

* 영어는 우리말로, 우리말은 영어로 써 보세요.

1. nature _____   2. brick _____

3. important _____   4. adventure _____

5. arrow _____   6. 마지막의 _____

7. 의미하다 _____   8. 커튼 _____

9. 기원, 근원 _____   10. 남자 배우 _____

* 우리말과 같은 뜻이 되도록 빈칸을 채워보세요.

11. Don't _____ the cheese too long. 치즈를 오랫동안 굽지 마라.

12. She knows the desert _____ very well.
    그녀는 그 사막 지역을 아주 잘 알고 있다.

13. Both sugar and salt _____ in water. 설탕과 소금 모두 물에 녹는다.

14. His father worked for a big _____.
    그의 아버지는 큰 회사에서 근무했다.

15. Do you _____ live at the same address?
    당신은 아직 같은 주소에 사세요?

* 단어의 뜻에 맞게 빈칸에 알맞은 단어를 쓰세요.

16. _____ : a measurement between two points

17. _____ : something that is given to another person

Test 15 정답 | 1. 우수한, 탁월한 2. 지루한 3. 만지다 4. 이웃 5. 마침내 6. hunt 7. guess 8. difference 9. sharp 10. roof
11. collected 12. foreign 13. simple 14. honest 15. straw 16. power 17. picnic

Answers

Spelling Bee 180

1. cold 2. afraid 3. write 4. wait 5. dollar 6. friend 7. pull 8. desk 9. away 10. after 11. square 12. weak 13. cook 14. become 15. call 16. put 17. summer 18. run 19. full 20. eye 21. sell 22. hungry 23. ready 24. cow 25. chopsticks 26. pay 27. sky 28. thirsty 29. week 30. marry 31. south 32. shop 33. through 34. luck 35. hot 36. wake 37. large 38. picture 39. die 40. thank 41. sorry 42. fast 43. free 44. bread 45. answer 46. zoo 47. money 48. queen 49. count 50. sour 51. ill 52. news 53. smart 54. know 55. ugly 56. tired 57. all 58. market 59. chalk 60. find 61. laugh 62. student 63. piano 64. west 65. bird 66. push 67. flower 68. big 69. minute 70. green 71. chair 72. work 73. fly 74. woman 75. chest 76. clothes 77. clock 78. wear 79. dentist 80. teach 81. light 82. sad 83. cup 84. bean 85. snake 86. field 87. jam 88. shoe 89. bring 90. left 91. seat 92. dish 93. wash 94. boat 95. love 96. egg 97. clean 98. bowl 99. soap 100. early 101. evening 102. country 103. thin 104. train 105. sandwich 106. doctor 107. house 108. grandmother 109. meat 110. finger 111. water 112. store 113. airplane 114. fat 115. lady 116. hobby 117. socks 118. quick 119. rich 120. expensive 121. neck 122. movie 123. sick 124. dry 125. boot 126. table 127. dance 128. world 129. music 130. bell 131. north 132. grow 133. long 134. mirror 135. sea 136. cloud 137. family 138. letter 139. visit 140. year 141. follow 142. nose 143. cut 144. learn 145. sit 146. catch 147. listen 148. pass 149. corner 150. stairs 151. street 152. buy 153. kitchen 154. garden 155. warm 156. night 157. cute 158. noon 159. song 160. use 161. problem 162. tennis 163. hundred 164. vegetable 165. begin 166. candy 167. ride 168. want 169. hospital 170. food 171. fall 172. person 173. land 174. telephone 175. change 176. absent 177. understand 178. angry 179. worry 180. best

Spelling Bee 100

1. ticket 2. woods 3. drum 4. steal 5. math 6. twins 7. lake 8. dead 9. heart 10. deer 11. lie 12. appear 13. ghost 14. famous 15. present 16. bench 17. explain 18. patient 19. forgive 20. fact 21. kite 22. quarrel 23. fire 24. soldier 25. ground 26. butter 27. clever 28. feather 29. mailman 30. prince 31. wise 32. beach 33. birthday 34. decide 35. plan 36. bone 37. punish 38. sound 39. palace 40. ice 41. travel 42. classmate 43. wet 44. spider 45. wood 46. boil 47. camera 48. wild 49. album 50. thief 51. library 52. voice 53. matter 54. danger 55. save 56. freedom 57. dictionary 58. fill 59. hill 60. skin 61. hunt 62. theater 63. foreign 64. mistake 65. steam 66. museum 67. collect 68. popular 69. power 70. law 71. angel 72. boring 73. health 74. touch 75. special 76. science 77. neighbor 78. succeed 79. exam 80. education 81. feel 82. discover 83. straw 84. raise 85. nature 86. machine 87. break 88. wave 89. brick 90. mix 91. lock 92. area 93. melt 94. chance 95. shadow 96. origin 97. cage 98. company 99. view 100. job